Smokelore

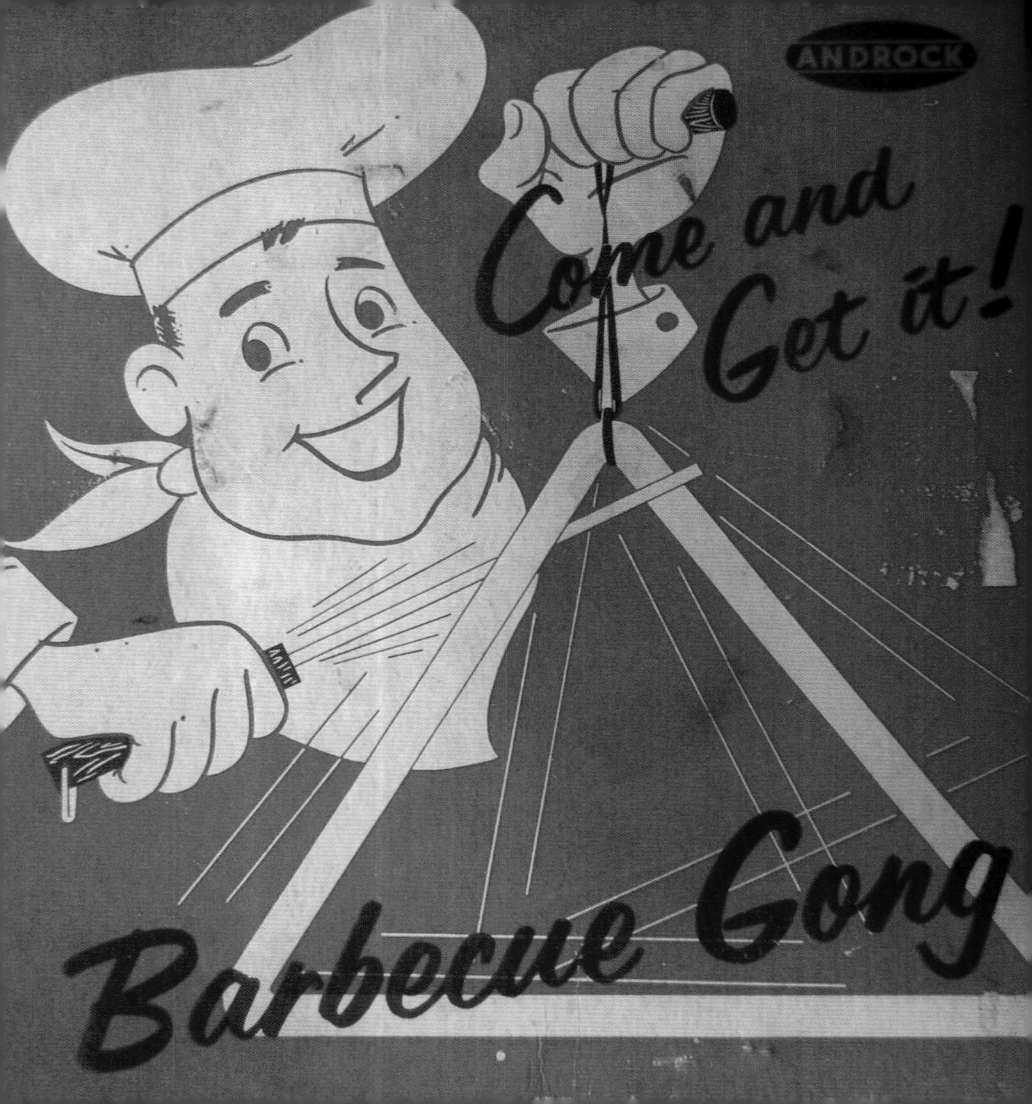
ANDROCK
Come and Get it!
Barbecue Gong

SMOKE LORE

A SHORT HISTORY OF BARBECUE IN AMERICA 🔥 JIM AUCHMUTEY

THE UNIVERSITY OF GEORGIA PRESS   ATHENS

Published by the University of Georgia Press
Athens, Georgia 30602
www.ugapress.org
© 2019 by Jim Auchmutey
All rights reserved
Designed by Erin Kirk New
Set in Miller Text
Printed and bound by Versa Press
The paper in this book meets the guidelines for
permanence and durability of the Committee on
Production Guidelines for Book Longevity of the
Council on Library Resources.

Most University of Georgia Press titles are
available from popular e-book vendors.

Printed in the United States of America
23 22 21 20 19 P 5 4 3 2 1

Library of Congress Cataloging-in-Publication Data
Names: Auchmutey, Jim, author.
Title: Smokelore : a short history of barbecue in America /
    Jim Auchmutey.
Description: Athens : University of Georgia Press, [2019] |
    Includes bibliographical references and index.
Identifiers: LCCN 2018057926 | ISBN 9780820338415 (pbk. :
    alk. paper)
Subjects: LCSH: Barbecuing—United States—History. |
    Barbecuing—United States—Anecdotes.
Classification: LCC TX840.B3 A92 2019 | DDC 641.7/60973—
    dc23 LC record available at https://lccn.loc.gov/2018057926

Page vii: The pink neon pig of the
Auburn Avenue Rib Shack beckoned for years
in downtown Atlanta. When the restaurant
closed in 1994, the sign was preserved at the
Atlanta History Center museum.

This publication was made possible

in part by a generous contribution from

Thomas and Catherine Fleetwood

and by

The Bradley Hale Fund

for Southern Studies

FOR PAM

CONTENTS

ACKNOWLEDGMENTS

I started researching this book when I was about five years old. My mother would take the family to Lefty's, a drive-in restaurant run by a former semipro baseball pitcher near our home in Decatur, Georgia. We'd sit in our green '53 Chevy and order curb service, the windows down because the car lacked air-conditioning. As we waited, we could smell the pork cooking over hickory smoke. Waiting. Smelling. Waiting. Smelling. I could have taken a bite out of the backseat. I was hooked on barbecue before I began kindergarten. I'd like to thank my mother, Janey Yarbrough Auchmutey, for starting me out right.

My father's side of the family continued my barbecue education. As I mention in the introduction, my grandfather, Bob Auchmutey, was a respected pitmaster in Bartow County, Georgia. Our dog-eared copy of a 1954 *Saturday Evening Post* that featured him in a story about southern barbecue was a family heirloom when I was growing up. But it wasn't just Daddy Bob. My father, Charles Auchmutey, was a skilled Brunswick stew maker, as was his younger brother, my uncle Earl. When Earl came to visit, he often stopped for takeout at a barbecue place on the way to Atlanta—usually Stodgehill's or Fresh Air, in the Jackson area. He'd walk into our house bearing that fragrant bundle, cracking wise. Earl was the uncle who'd tell my brother and me dirty jokes. I've associated barbecue with fun ever since.

In my first decade as a reporter and editor at the *Atlanta Journal-Constitution*, I occasionally wrote articles about food, but it was never my focus. That began to change in 1990 when I met our new food editor, Susan Puckett. With Susan's encouragement, I came to

OPPOSITE: A decommissioned sign for a Pig 'n Whistle barbecue drive-in, for sale in 2010 at an antique dealer in Atlanta. The sign was later claimed by a man who wants to relaunch the barbecue chain.

see that food was a rich vein of cultural anthropology, and my interest in the subject grew and deepened. We wrote two cookbooks together, including, in 1995, *The Ultimate Barbecue Sauce Cookbook*. Thank you, Susan, for being such a dear friend and trusted colleague.

This book grew out of the Atlanta History Center's 2018–19 exhibition about the history and culture of barbecue, Barbecue Nation. Michael Rose, the museum's chief mission officer, pulled me into the project in stages. In 2008, when I was still working at the *Journal-Constitution*, he asked me to be an advisor. Then he and the History Center's publishing partner, the University of Georgia Press, asked me to write the companion volume. Finally, the History Center hired me to be a guest curator for the exhibition when the show reached fruition a decade after I first became involved. Thank you, Michael, for getting me into this predicament.

I want to express appreciation to my other colleagues at the History Center, among them: Don Rooney, Jonathan Scott, Jena Jones, Calinda Lee, Hillary Hardwick, Howard Pousner, Kate Whitman, and Sheffield Hale. I'd like to especially acknowledge Craig Pascoe, a history professor at Georgia State College & University who served as curator of the exhibition for years before I was asked to step in. Craig loves barbecue so much that he's launched a Georgia barbecue website (www.georgiabbqtrails) and founded a state chapter of the Campaign for Real Barbecue, recognizing barbecue joints that still cook over wood.

The book and exhibition would not have happened without the contributions of barbecue lovers and collectors across the country. Thank heaven for Ed Reilly, the Weber sales rep, who is a one-man barbecue archivist. And Ardie Davis, aka Remus Powers, a barbecue historian of the first rank who has a particular affinity for vintage postcards. And Carolyn Wells, cofounder of the Kansas City Barbeque Society, who brought her expertise as an advisor to the exhibition. And Jessica Harris, another advisor, who offered valuable insights about the multicultural roots of barbecue. And John Shelton Reed and Dale Volberg Reed, who proudly documented North Carolina's crucial role in the barbecue story. And Daniel Vaughn of *Texas Monthly*, Robert Moss of *Southern Living*, Jim Shahin of the *Washington Post*, and Craig "Meathead" Goldwyn of *AmazingRibs .com*, who were all helpful and generous with their input.

Many thanks to John T. Edge and the Southern Foodways Alliance at the University of Mississippi, who have been supportive of this book and exhibition for years. And to the editors and production staff who have shepherded the project at the University of Georgia Press, especially Patrick Allen, who kept things rolling during our several stops and starts.

I'm especially indebted to the many barbecue restaurants and businesses who cherish their legacy and share it with others. You are curators of an important part of our culinary history.

Finally, I'd like to thank my wife, Pamela Brown Auchmutey, who has shared my food adventures for more than forty years of marriage. She loves barbecue almost as much as I do and has the wisdom to realize that her husband does not need to own every pig knickknack sold—only the really clever ones.

Smokelore

Introduction

I've always wondered why we say something is as American as apple pie. Nothing against apple pie, but history tells us that apples came from Asia by way of Europe and that the British fancied baking them into pies long before anyone on this side of the Atlantic did. If you're looking for a food that truly represents the New World, you would be hard pressed to find a better one than barbecue.

In a sense, America began with a barbecue.

On September 18, 1793, less than a decade after the United States was constituted, George Washington boarded a boat near his Virginia plantation and sailed up the Potomac River for the "federal city," as he called the newly designated seat of government. His destination was a hilltop where workers had broken ground on a grand public building. The first president was going to lay the very foundation of American democracy, the cornerstone of the Capitol.

Once ashore, Washington joined a procession of officials and military men as they marched in a solemn procession to the site. The president, wearing an ornate Masonic apron, descended into a trench at the southeastern corner of the excavation and began the rituals of the ancient fraternal order. He placed three symbolic substances on the cornerstone in sequence—corn, wine, oil—and called for God's blessing after each, as the other Masons looking on chanted in response. Then Washington laid an engraved silver plate on the block, and a battery of artillery fired a volley. When the consecration was done, the party moved on to another ritual that was already becoming a tradition in the young nation.

They held a barbecue.

OPPOSITE: George Washington dedicating the cornerstone of the U.S. Capitol in 1793, as depicted in a 1950s mural by Allyn Cox at the George Washington Masonic National Memorial in Alexandria, Virginia. Barbecue was involved.

By the time he presided over that ceremony, Washington was an old hand at barbecue. As a prominent member of the Virginia gentry, he had been attending plantation barbecues most of his life and mentions them half a dozen times in his diaries, sometimes even spelling the word correctly. But the American way of barbecue far predates the Father of His Country. It goes back almost three hundred years before the founding of the republic to the earliest encounters between European explorers and native peoples in the Caribbean.

"Barbecue" is the English version of a Spanish word describing an Indian cooking technique that took root in the South, where it was prized by planters and usually prepared by African Americans, and eventually spread throughout the United States. It is America in a mouthful. The story of barbecue touches almost every aspect of our history. It involves the age of discovery, the colonial era, slavery, the Civil War, the settling of the West, the coming of immigrants, the Great Migration of blacks and whites from the South, the rise of the automobile, the expansion of suburbia, the rejiggering of gender roles. It encompasses every region and demographic group. It is entwined with our politics and tangled up with our race relations.

If barbecue were a movie, it would be an epic with the sweep of Cecil B. DeMille, the sauciness of Robert Altman, and the irreverence of Spike Lee. There would be cameo appearances by stars like Christopher Columbus, Andrew Jackson, Abraham Lincoln, Buffalo Bill, Henry Ford, Louis Armstrong, Elvis Presley, Martin Luther King Jr., and Richard Petty (who, being a North Carolinian, felt compelled to step off the racetrack long enough to peddle his own line of barbecue sauces). The cast list could go on; did I mention Homer Simpson?

Of course, most barbecue history has been made by less-renowned people: the generations of pitmasters, backyard cooks, and barbecue-stand operators who refined and perpetuated the craft. I'm proud to say that one of them was my grandfather Charles Robert Auchmutey Sr., a farmer-turned-fireman who supervised the barbecue and made the Brunswick stew at community gatherings in the Etowah River valley of northwest Georgia. Daddy Bob, as we called him, would have remained a local figure if the *Saturday Evening Post* hadn't

Robert Auchmutey was in great demand after the *Saturday Evening Post* featured him in a 1954 article about southern barbecue. Shortly afterward, he posed with his pit crew. That's Daddy Bob (as the family knew him) second from right. Uncle Earl's on the far left.

published an article about barbecue on the weekend of the Fourth of July in 1954. The writer was from Georgia and set the story in Bartow County, where my grandfather ran the pit at the Euharlee Farmers Club barbecue. The first picture in the five-page spread shows him staring down into a smoky trench lined with pig and lamb carcasses, his grave countenance leaving little doubt that he took his duties as seriously as a schoolmaster. The magazine called him a "barbecue chef." I imagine that highfalutin title elicited some snickers down at the fire station.

After the article appeared, a civic group in Park Forest, Illinois, invited my grandfather to the Chicago area to cook barbecue and stew for a multitude of two thousand people. Six Georgians made the journey in two cars loaded with cast-iron washpots and other equipment essential to the task. When he returned home, Daddy Bob recounted their experiences to the local paper in a story that ran under the tongue-in-cheek headline "Rebels Cook Southern 'Cue in Very Midst of Yankeeland." I'm not sure he had ever been to Yankeeland. That barbecue road trip was one of the biggest adventures of his life.

All of which is to say that barbecue is more than a food to me. It's personal. It's about where we came from and who we are. It's about families and friends and the fond memories that envelop so many of us when we catch a whiff of hardwood smoke.

I wrote this book because I wanted to complete the circle that takes in George Washington and Bob Auchmutey and all the others, past and present, famous and obscure, whose love of barbecue has made it one of the most authentic expressions of our culture, right up there with jazz and baseball—something universal, yet uniquely American.

I'm well aware that the world is eaten up with barbecue books. If you search Amazon, you'll find thousands and thousands of titles. There are legions of cookbooks and quite a few guides, not to mention photo collections, scholarly treatments, explorations of regional styles, and the occasional mystery or romance (*Cooking in the Nude: For Barbecue Buffs*—hey, why not?). A very few of the books deal with barbecue history. This one differs in that it's an *illustrated* history, relying as much on vintage images as text, in keeping with its inspiration as the companion volume to Barbecue Nation, an exhibition about the food and its culture organized by the Atlanta History Center. Think of this book, then, as a guided tour of barbecue's past, with lots of snapshots and props, some of them quite amusing. It's meant to be fun. We're talking about barbecue, folks.

Before we set out, there's one scrap of unfinished business. You might wonder what sort of barbecue Washington and the other worthies ate after that cornerstone dedication in 1793. While there's no doubt who cooked the meat—slaves, of course—little is known about the menu. But there is a record of the main course. In the only contemporary account, a newspaper called the *Columbian Mirror and Alexandrian Gazette* reported that the founding feasters dined on a five-hundred-pound ox. In other words, the centerpiece of the first great barbecue in the nation's capital was not pork but beef—and Texas wasn't even part of the Union yet.

They had no idea how debated such distinctions would become.

The broyling of their fish ouer the flame of fier.

nᴮ

1

The Smoke of a Distant Shore

The first recorded barbecue in the Americas didn't feature ribs or brisket or pulled pork. It involved a main course that was so alien some of the guests were left gagging—which probably served them right, since they weren't guests as much as intruders.

It happened on April 30, 1494, during Christopher Columbus's second voyage to the New World. The Admiral of the Ocean Sea was sailing along the coast of a large island that he assumed was part of Asia but that was actually what would later become known as Cuba. When the ships entered Guantánamo Bay, the men spotted fires along the shore and, as they drew closer, sniffed an appetizing scent. A landing party was dispatched and discovered fish and an unfamiliar reptilian creature cooking on some sort of spit.

"In many places there were many serpents, the most disgusting and nauseating things which the men ever saw, all with their mouths sewn up," Spanish historian Andrés Bernáldez wrote in an early account of the voyage. "From the head to the tip of the tail, down the middle of the back, they had long projections, disgusting, and sharp as the points of diamonds. The admiral ordered the fish to be taken, and with it refreshed his men."

The mystery meat they wouldn't touch was iguana. Never having seen the spiky lizards, the Spaniards thought them loathsome. When some of the natives finally arrived on the scene, they seemed relieved that the iguana was still there, for they considered it a delicacy. They were preparing a feast for a visiting chieftain, smoking the meat on a raised grid of green branches that explorers would observe throughout the Caribbean in the coming years. The natives

an expedition from Tampa Bay and saw Indians using barbacoas on the North American mainland, showing that they weren't just a Caribbean contrivance. A quarter of a century later, a Frenchman in northern Florida made the first illustrations of barbacoa cooking in what became the United States. The age of exploration was a cruel time, and both precedents are splattered with blood.

The Spanish arrived in 1539 with a small army led by the conquistador Hernando de Soto. They came ashore near present-day Bradenton with some six hundred men, more than two hundred horses, and a small herd of swine—the first on American soil. Over the next four years, the soldiers traveled four thousand miles through the Southeast looking for gold, slaves, and empire. As they slashed their way into the interior, the Spanish observed barbacoas used for storage and cooking; accounts of the journey use both senses of the word.

Perhaps the first published reference to "barbacoa" in English comes from one of these chronicles, a 1611 translation of a Spanish narrative extravagantly titled *The Worthye and Famous History of the Travailes, Discovery & Conquest of that great Continent of Terra Florida*. It describes a battle in middle Florida in which the invaders chased an Indian "to a loft made of canes, which they build to keep their maiz in, which they call a barbacoa, and there hee made such a noise, as though ten men had been defending the doore." The soldiers killed the poor native right there in the barbacoa.

A less distressing scene unfolded later on the Ocmulgee River, in central Georgia, where De Soto's men came upon a village and helped themselves to wild turkey and venison roasting on a barbacoa. "This was the first barbecue in Georgia to be recorded in the annals of history," wrote De Soto historian Charles M. Hudson.

Every winter, National Park Service rangers demonstrate the Indian way of grilling at the De Soto National Memorial in Bradenton. They erect a twenty-first-century barbacoa—four posts supporting a grid of palmetto fronds stripped of foliage—and smoke some fish and chicken quarters over yellow-pine coals (not the best for barbecuing, but the Timucuan people didn't have much hardwood). The tourists love it. "A lot of visitors are surprised to find out that barbecue was a Native American invention," says ranger Dan Stephens, who makes sure that they understand the connection between the Indians' rudimentary grills and the shiny store-bought versions most Americans fire up on the deck.

BARBACOA TODAY

There are almost as many signs for barbacoa as barbecue in parts of southern Texas. Visitors who think the former is simply a translation of the latter soon discover that they are mistaken; *barbacoa* is definitely not Spanish for American barbecue.

When the first Europeans came to the New World, the word referred to a framework of sticks that the natives used to cook food, store things to keep them off the ground, or even sleep upon. Now it refers to a dish in Latin America and the southwestern United States.

A barbacoa place in San Antonio, Texas, 1994.

In classic barbacoa, whole cows, goats, or sheep—or sometimes just their heads—are slow-roasted and steamed in a hole dug in the ground and covered with green leaves. It's usually cooked in an oven these days, using smaller cuts, the meat pulled off and served in a taco or tortilla. The Chipotle restaurant chain uses barbacoa in this sense as the name for the spicy shredded beef it sells at its thousands of outlets.

Twenty-five years after De Soto, another European arrived in Florida with drastically different motives. Jacques Le Moyne was the first professional artist known to have visited North America for the purpose of documenting Indians and their natural world. He came in 1564 with an expedition of French Huguenots charged with establishing a Protestant colony somewhere on the southeastern coast. They founded Fort Caroline on the St. Johns River, in today's Jacksonville, and Le Moyne went to work illustrating the local natives. One of his more familiar images shows two men loading a frightful smorgasbord of snakes, alligators, dogs, and other critters onto a sturdy barbacoa. The cooking grid looks a little high to modern eyes, the fire much too big for slow-cooking. If the particulars seem less than accurate, there's good reason.

Le Moyne barely escaped Florida with his life. Soldiers from the Spanish town of St. Augustine, thirty miles to the south, attacked the French and massacred all but two dozen of the people living at the fort. The artist made it back to France, but his drawings and journals

At the De Soto National Memorial in Bradenton, Florida, visitors can watch re-creations of the way indigenous people cooked on barbacoas.

A Seminole woman grilling turtle in the old way at the Florida Folk Life Festival, 1987.

were probably destroyed. He eventually settled in London, where he re-created his lost work from memory. Only one of his original American paintings survives, and some scholars have questioned its authenticity. The barbacoa tableau is an engraving based on a reconstruction and therefore several steps removed from its source.

Toward the end of his life, Le Moyne met a young artist who became something of a protégé and would become known for his own participation in a doomed colony. The younger man also created the second drawing of an Indian barbacoa, this time in the heart of what would become southern barbecue country.

John White was part of Sir Walter Raleigh's attempt to establish a British colony on the coast of North Carolina, in 1585. White went along as an artist and mapmaker, painting dozens of watercolors depicting the Croatan Indians in a simple, naturalistic style. His barbacoa resembles the one Le Moyne sketched in Florida, but it appears to be smaller, and instead of a menagerie of exotic game, there are only two blue-tinted fish on the slats, "broyling . . . over the

Planked Salmon

If you want a glimpse of the earliest cooking techniques that led to American barbecue, think fish. The indigenous peoples of the New World cooked everything from trout and walleye to shad and salmon over fire and smoke. You can see throwbacks to this tradition on both coasts—in Essex, Connecticut, where they hold an annual shad bake, nailing the fish to oak planks propped around a fire, and in Neah Bay, Washington, where the Makah tribe ties butterflied salmon to cedar or alder stakes and cooks it around a bed of coals. Steven Raichlen, the cookbook author and TV barbecue host, has witnessed both. In his 2003 book *BBQ USA* he offered this recipe for a domesticated version of planked salmon. The cedar imparts an aromatic flavor to the fish.

FOR THE SALMON

1 cedar plank, about 6 by 12 inches
1 salmon fillet, with or without skin, about 1½ pounds
1 tablespoon olive oil
Coarse salt to taste
Freshly ground black pepper to taste
Dill sprigs, for garnish

FOR THE GLAZE

½ cup mayonnaise
⅓ cup grainy mustard
2 tablespoons chopped fresh dill
½ teaspoon finely grated lemon zest
Coarse salt to taste
Freshly ground black pepper to taste

Soak the plank in water for at least 45 minutes. Brush the skin side of the salmon with olive oil and season both sides with salt and pepper. Place the fillet, skin side down, on the cedar plank.

Make the glaze by combining all ingredients in a small mixing bowl. Spread the glaze evenly over the top of the salmon.

Build a fire in your charcoal grill, or preheat your gas grill to medium-high. Place the plank with the fish on the grate, away from direct heat, and grill for 15 minutes, until the internal temperature reads 135° to 140°F. The glaze should be a deep golden brown. Garnish with dill sprigs and serve directly off the plank.

flame—they took great heed that they bee not burntt." There are no people in the painting, and White does not mention what they call their cooker.

The first colony on Roanoke Island failed. White was appointed governor of a second attempted colony, but that one fared no better. He returned to England for supplies, leaving a hundred people behind, and by the time he made it back across the Atlantic, everyone had vanished into the wilderness—including his granddaughter, Virginia Dare, the first English person born in North America. The legend of the Lost Colony was born.

Theodor de Bry used early illustrations to make engravings of New World barbecues in the late 1500s. He took considerable artistic license.

Ein höltzern Roost/darauff sie die
Fische besengen.   XIIII.

Ann sie eine grosse menge Fische haben gefangen/begeben sie sich auff einen därzu verordneten Platz/welcher die Speiß zu bereiten bequeme ist/daselbst stecken sie vier Gabeln auff einem viereckten Platz in die Erden hinein/auff diese legen sie vier Höltzer/vnd auff dieselbigen andere zwerchsweise/also/daß es einem Roost/der da hoch gnugsam sey/gleichförmig werde. Wann sie die Fische auff den Roost gelegt/machen sie ein Fewer darunter/doch nicht nach der weise der Völcker von Florida/welche die Fisch allein besengen/vnnd im Rauch außtrücknen/die sie den gantzen Winter vber behalten. Diese Völcker aber braten alles/verzehrens/vñ behalten nichts in vorraht/darnach/wann sie dessen dörfftig sind/braten oder sieden sie frische/wie wir hernach sehen werden. Wann aber der Roost so groß nicht ist/daß die Fisch alle möchten darauff gelegt werden/stecken sie kleine stecklein am Fewer in die Erden/vnnd hencken die vbrigen Fische durch die Ohren auff/vnd braten sie vollendt so lang es gnug sey. Sie sehen aber mit fleiß zu/daß sie nicht verbrennt werden. Wann die ersten gebraten sind/legen sie andere/so sie frisch herzu gebracht/auff den Roost. Vnd also widerholen sie diß braten so lange/biß sie der Speise gnugsam zu haben vermeynen.

Easy Barbacoa

Eddie Hernandez, the chef at the popular Taqueria del Sol restaurants in Atlanta, grew up with barbacoa in Mexico. His uncle José would put beef inside a large can, bury it in the ground with a bed of coals, cover it with agave leaves, and let it cook all day. An impatient man, his nephew wanted to find an easier way that didn't require him to, as he puts it, "dig a friggin' hole in his yard." His solution: slow-cooker barbacoa. Hernandez moved to Texas as a young man and discovered the pleasures of American barbecue, but he never stopped loving Mexican barbacoa. This recipe comes from *Turnip Greens & Tortillas*, his 2018 cookbook with Susan Puckett.

Makes 16 to 20 servings

¼ cup salt

1 tablespoon ground black pepper

8 bay leaves

5 pounds beef brisket, cut to fit in a large slow cooker

5 pounds beef cheeks, cut to fit in a large slow cooker

(*Note:* You usually have to special-order beef cheeks from a butcher. You can make this recipe with nothing but brisket, but Hernandez recommends using cheek meat as well for its intense flavor.)

In a large bowl, combine the salt, pepper, and bay leaves. Add the meat and toss to combine. Place in a large slow cooker, cover and set on low. Cook for 12 hours or overnight, until the meat is falling apart. Skim the grease and remove the fatty pieces and bone. Discard the bay leaves. Shred the meat and serve on a platter with tortillas and salsa, garnished with lime wedges, chopped cilantro, and chopped red onion.

The fact that White's artwork didn't vanish as well is owed to the efforts of a man who never traveled to the New World. Theodor de Bry was a Flemish engraver who met White and Le Moyne in London during the 1580s and arranged to use their paintings as the basis for copperplate images he included in a series of books about exploration called *Great Voyages*. The volumes were hugely popular—the *National Geographic*s of their time—in part because De Bry didn't hesitate to alter images in an effort to appeal to a broader audience. No one knows how he changed Le Moyne's painting because the original did not survive. But he added a couple of Indians to White's scene and pumped up their muscles to make them look like something out of a Michelangelo sculpture.

Soon De Bry put the barbacoa to a more sinister purpose. In 1592 he used the artists' Indian cookers as a template to illustrate an account of cannibalism in South America, replacing their fish and game with human arms and legs, severed for the grill.

If De Bry made barbecue seem barbaric, he wasn't alone. Many colonial writers associated barbecue with the wild ways of the newfound hemisphere and its indigenous people. Surveying the early uses of the term, Andrew Warnes in his 2008 book *Savage Barbecue* went so far as to say that barbecue was as much the creation of a fevered European imagination as an indigenous American cooking technique. The *Oxford English Dictionary*'s citation for the first published use of "barbecue" in the language underscores the argument; it isn't something you'd want to read over a plate of ribs. "Jamaica Viewed," a 1661 travelogue by a British clergyman named Edmund Hickeringill who had lived on the island, had this to say about the dining customs of the Carib Indians, who gave their name to the Caribbean:

> But usually their slaves, when Captive ta'en,
> Are to the English sold, and some are Slain,
> And their Flesh forthwith Barbacu'd and Eat
> By them, their Wives and Children as choice Meat.

Along the same lines, several of the dictionary's earliest references to barbecue have to do with people being roasted alive. Aphra Behn, one of the first women in England to become a professional writer, used the word somewhat jokingly in her 1690 play *The Widdow Ranter* as a Virginia lynch mob demands to get its hands on a prisoner, yelling, "Let's barbicu this fat Rogue." Cotton Mather, the Puritan clergyman, meant it literally in his 1702 history *Magnalia Christi Americana* as he described New Englanders setting fire to the lodges of Narragansett Indians, who were "terribly Barbikew'd."

(Notice the erratic spelling. "Barbecue" didn't become the standard until Samuel Johnson's landmark dictionary in 1755, and even after that, people continued to write it every which way. Webster agrees with Johnson, and I wouldn't want to argue with either of them— hence the spelling in this book.)

Despite the metaphoric flourishes of clever writers, it's sensible to assume that for most people living in the Americas in the 1600s

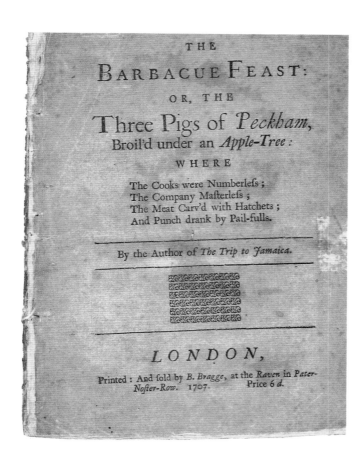

THE

BARBACUE FEAST:

OR, THE

Three Pigs of *Peckham*,
Broil'd under an *Apple-Tree* :

WHERE

The Cooks were Numberlefs ;
The Company Mafterlefs ;
The Meat Carv'd with Hatchets ;
And Punch drank by Pail-fulls.

By the Author of *The Trip to Jamaica.*

LONDON,

Printed : And fold by *B. Bragge*, at the *Raven* in *Pater-
Nofter-Row.* 1707. Price 6 *d.*

The Barbacue Feast provided the first description of a real barbecue in the English language in 1707.

and early 1700s, "barbecue" referred to a cooking system and not a means for roasting people alive, whether for punishment or nourishment. Somewhere along the way, the word came to mean by extension a social gathering at which a barbecue meal was the centerpiece. When did this happen? The best clue is a pamphlet that appeared in London in 1707, "The Barbacue Feast: or, the Three Pigs of Peckham, Broil'd under an Apple-Tree." It may be the first full description of a barbecue in the modern sense.

The scene is again Jamaica, in the town of Peckham, where writer Edward Ward said he witnessed a group of rum-sotted English colonists take a walk on the wild side at a bacchanal centered around "a Litter of Pigs most nicely cook'd after the West-India manner." The pigs smoked for hours, the cook basting them with Madeira wine applied with a rustic mop made of a fox's tail attached to a stick. The pork began to change color, Ward wrote, "and looked as brown on the Scabboard side, as the tawny Belly of an Indian Squaw, just painted over with yellow oker and Bears-grease, so that warm Disputes arose amongst the crowding Spectators, whether it was, or was not, high time to take 'em by the Hocks, and give 'em a Turn upon the Grid-Iron."

Barbecue, it seems, was always the subject of warm disputes.

Ward spun an entertaining yarn, but he wasn't much help for readers who actually wanted to learn how to cook a pig in the "West-India manner." Aspiring pitmasters had to wait until 1732 when the first known barbecue recipe appeared in an English guidebook with the chewy title *The Country Housewife and Lady's Director, in the Management of a House, and the Delights and Profits of a Farm.* The

The Country Housewife included the first barbecue recipe in 1732.

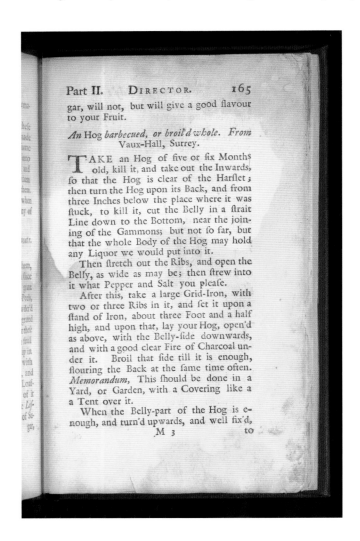

author, Richard Bradley, a Cambridge University botany professor who wrote about gardening and cooking, showed an enthusiasm for New World indulgences by including recipes for rum, snuff, and a pineapple tart (said to be the first pineapple recipe in English—a culinary pioneer, this one).

Bradley's contribution to smoke-cooking appears on page 165 in an entry headed "An Hog barbecued, or broil'd whole." The professor gave instructions for cleaning the hog and splitting and spreading it on a gridiron "with a Fire of Charcoal under it." Lest anyone think this kitchen work, he cautioned that "this should be done in a Yard, or Garden, with a Covering like a Tent over it." To season the pig's "gravy," he suggested a sort of basting sauce: "three or four Quarts of Water, and half as much White-Wine, and as much Salt as you will, with some Sage cut small; adding the Peels of six or eight Lemons, and an Ounce of fresh Cloves whole." Cooking time: seven to eight hours.

Sounds pretty good.

Adventuresome British cooks probably welcomed Bradley's advice. But in the colonies, one imagines, they hardly needed a Cambridge don to tell them how to barbecue. By that time, they were well on their way to turning the Indian barbacoa into something different and utterly American.

2

The Cradle

There must be a dozen places in the United States that claim to be the capital of barbecue—most of them in the South—but only one feels so strongly about it that someone went to the trouble of backing up the boast with a photogenic work of vernacular architecture. In Ayden, North Carolina, a town of five thousand in the flat tobacco country east of Raleigh, one of the most storied barbecue restaurants in the nation, the Skylight Inn, features a shiny sheet-metal replica of the U.S. Capitol dome on its roof with Old Glory rippling from the top. In case anyone misses the point, a billboard across the parking lot declares this "The Bar-B-Q Capital of the World."

An orator once described North Carolina as a vale of humility between two mountains of conceit: its history-proud neighbors Virginia and South Carolina. When it comes to barbecue, that reputation for comparative humility does not hold. North Carolina regularly proclaims itself the cradle, if not quite the birthplace, of American barbecue.

That qualifier refers to Virginia, where the cultural merging that led to barbecue first took place, given that it was settled decades before North Carolina. The indigenous people of the Tidewater region cooked on the same sort of barbacoa framework that explorers had encountered in the Caribbean. English settlers brought pigs and a taste for pork and, starting in 1619, enslaved Africans who usually tended the pits and stirred things up with new spices and peppers. "The only unbroken line of southern barbecue history begins in Virginia," wrote Joseph R. Haynes in his book *Virginia Barbecue: A History.*

OPPOSITE: The Skylight Inn in Ayden, North Carolina, smokes whole hogs and serves them with a spicy vinegar sauce, carrying on one of the oldest traditions in American barbecue.

Despite such assertions, North Carolina usually gets more attention for its barbecue pedigree. Perhaps people there care more about it, John Shelton Reed and Dale Volberg Reed suggest in *Holy Smoke*, their history of Tar Heel barbecue. "Virginians were distracted by hams and Brunswick stew, leaving North Carolina in undisputed possession of the longest continuous barbecue tradition on the North American mainland."

Undisputed? Let the record show that some people in South Carolina believe *they* were first. Barbecue historian Lake E. High Jr. argued that his state, not the ones to the north, was the site of the earliest true barbecue on the continent, dating to the late 1500s and the failed Spanish colony of Santa Elena, on the coast. "During the twenty-one years the Spanish were in Santa Elena," he wrote in *A History of South Carolina Barbeque*, "a wonderful thing happened: barbeque was born!" The state tourism bureau ran with it and advertised South Carolina on its website as "the birthplace of barbecue." (They agreed on the spiel but not on the spelling.)

The claims and opinions can get confusing. Whatever you make of them, one thing is clear: American barbecue as we know it took shape on the southeastern seaboard. This is where it sank its taproot, where it acquired its southern accent. This is where it began.

By 1757, when this Presbyterian church near Sanford, North Carolina, was founded, barbecue had become such a fixture that it appeared in place-names.

On a country lane between Sanford and Fort Bragg, in central North Carolina, there's a history marker that road foodies like to pull over and photograph. "Barbecue Church," it says, summoning visions of pork worshippers chanting before a brick pit altar. The truth is more prosaic: the sign refers to Barbecue Presbyterian Church, whose sanctuary on Barbecue Church Road is the latest home of a congregation founded by Highland Scots in 1757. The name comes from Barbecue Creek, which got *its* name when a settler saw mist rising off the water and thought it looked like the smoke he had seen at pig roasts in the Caribbean. Barbecue must have been on people's minds because there was also a Barbecue Swamp in North Carolina and another in Virginia and a "Barbycue Branch" near the James River.

The earliest mentions of barbecue in the Carolinas and Virginia sound less like the smoking pits we know and more like campfire cooking. John Lawson, an English explorer who helped found some of the oldest towns in the Old North State, wrote in 1709 in *A New Voyage to Carolina* about natives who offered him "fat barbakued" venison and "roasted or barbakued turkey, eaten with Bears Fat."

THE MYSTERIES OF STEW

While southerners are united by their allegiance to barbecued pork, there's no consensus about sides. Hush puppies or white bread? Creamy coleslaw or vinegar slaw? On the sandwich or on the side? Each variation has its adherents and its home turf.

The longest-running debate about sides concerns stews. In South Carolina and bordering parts of Georgia, they serve barbecue hash, a pork paste made from remnants and offal, heaped over rice. For many, it's an acquired taste. In Kentucky they make a tangy stew from barbecued mutton, vegetables, and other meats called burgoo, a funny-sounding name of uncertain origin. It's the only barbecue specialty that ever won the Kentucky Derby; Burgoo King, a thoroughbred named for a renowned burgoo maker, took the 1932 race.

The most-disputed barbecue sidekick has to be Brunswick stew, which can be found in Virginia, Georgia, and sections of North Carolina—but not much of anywhere else. All three states claim to have originated the dish, which began as a hunter's stew containing squirrels and other critters. Virginia, having been settled first, makes the most convincing case, but that didn't stop Georgia from posting a historical marker on Interstate 95 proclaiming the town of Brunswick as the stew's birthplace.

Brunswick stew these days is made with chicken (Virginia), a mixture of meats (Georgia), or a hog's head (south Georgia). Some versions are loaded with vegetables, while others use only corn and tomatoes, leaving the stew as red as a muddy clay road.

My family has made Brunswick stew at gatherings in Georgia for more than a hundred years. Once, when I was helping my father cook a batch, I asked why we didn't use onions, lima beans, or other vegetables often seen in other stews. "Because your great-grandfather didn't, your grandfather didn't, and I don't," he replied, making it clear what was expected of me.

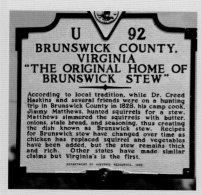

People in Virginia and Georgia enjoy quarreling over who created Brunswick stew. Virginia stakes its claim with a historical marker in Brunswick County, while Georgia has a stewpot monument on Interstate 95 near the city of Brunswick. Meanwhile, Kentucky is the uncontested homeland of a related stew, burgoo, which inspired the name of the 1932 Kentucky Derby winner Burgoo King.

A few years later, during the French and Indian War, George Washington spoke of barbecue as a means of preserving meat by smoking it. "We have not an ounce of salt provision of any kind here," he wrote in a 1758 dispatch requesting supplies for soldiers under his command, "and it is impossible to preserve the fresh . . . by any other means but barbacuing it in the Indian manner." When Washington mentioned barbecue again in his writings, in diary entries from the 1760s and '70s, he meant plantation social gatherings that could last for days—what he could have called barbecuing in the colonial manner.

An early indicator that Washington would soon be fighting against the British he had once served beside occurred in 1765 in Wilmington, North Carolina. It's the barbecue version of the Boston Tea Party, only it happened several years earlier. The British government had passed the Stamp Act, requiring colonists to buy stamps for all important documents, a despised measure that spawned the slogan No Taxation Without Representation. William Tryon, the crown's new governor in North Carolina, knew the people were riled and tried to appease them with a big public barbecue in Wilmington. But after he made a speech defending the Stamp Act, the crowd grew angry and ransacked the feast, smashing barrels of grog and stripping the barbecued ox that was to have been the highlight of the day.

Maybe the governor shouldn't have chosen beef. Pork had already become the preferred protein of colonial America because hogs were easy to raise, reproduced rapidly, and yielded a delicious meat that could literally be salted away. The taste for pig meat was especially pronounced in the southern colonies. When he visited North Carolina during the 1720s, Virginia planter William Byrd II disparaged the locals as lazy, coarse, and given to "gross humours" because they ate too much pork. "These People live so much upon Swine's flesh," he wrote, that it makes them "extremely hoggish in their Temper, & many of them seem to Grunt rather than Speak in their ordinary conversation."

Another outsider put it more diplomatically. Sara Hicks Williams, a New Yorker who married a North Carolina man and moved to his plantation, told her mother in a letter: "They esteem above all dishes . . . roasted pig dressed with red pepper and vinegar."

As southerners moved west into new territory, they took their love of pork and barbecue with them. One of the first places in the interior where the transplanted tradition flourished was Kentucky, once part of Virginia. The naturalist John James Audubon lived near Louisville around 1810 and later wrote a nostalgic reminiscence of an Independence Day barbecue he attended there. Another writer,

Southern Pork Shoulder

Pork shoulder is the workhorse of southern barbecue, pulled, chopped, or sliced, and served on plates or in sandwiches. The shoulder refers to the top portion of the hog's front leg and consists of two parts: the picnic ham, which is the lower cut, and the Boston butt, the upper cut. (The butt doesn't come from the butt; it gets its name from colonial days, when butchers in New England would pack it in barrels known as butts.) Most home cooks smoke a shoulder or butt, leaving the intricacies of whole hog barbecue to pitmasters. This recipe is adapted from John Shelton Reed's instructions in his 2016 book *Barbecue: A Savor the South Cookbook*.

1 pork shoulder
Southern Pork Rub to coat (see recipe below)

Apply rub generously to the pork shoulder. Let the meat sit in the refrigerator overnight. Light a charcoal fire in your cooker, using a starter chimney, with chunks of your favorite hardwood (usually hickory and oak) at hand. When the coals have burned down to a red-orange glow, place the meat on the grate, fat side up. Do not put the meat directly over the coals. If you're using an offset cooker, the fire will be in a separate chamber; if you're using a grill or a kettle cooker, keep the coals on one side and put the meat on the other, with a bowl of water over the coals to moisturize things. Or you can use a tower smoker, where a bowl of liquid sits between the meat rack on the top and the fire below.

The cooking will take at least 6 hours. Add coals to maintain a temperature of 210° to 250°F. Mop hourly if desired, but do not turn the meat. When the internal temperature reaches 180°F, remove the meat from the cooker, wrap it in heavy-duty foil, and let it rest for at least half an hour. Remove the bone, fat, and gristle, and slice, pull, or chop. If you pull or chop, be sure to mix the outside brown meat with the juicy inside meat.

SOUTHERN PORK RUB

Makes about 2 cups

1 cup paprika
½ cup packed light brown sugar
¼ cup kosher salt
2 tablespoons ground black pepper
2 tablespoons onion powder
1 tablespoon ground red pepper
1 tablespoon garlic powder
1 tablespoon dry mustard
1 tablespoon celery salt

Combine rub ingredients and mix well.

James Hall, has a character deliver this lecture about barbecue in his 1834 novel *Kentucky: A Tale*: "No taste for a barbecue! Well, that shows you were not raised in Virginia. Time you should see a little of the world, sir; there's nothing in life equal to a barbecue, properly managed—a good old Virginia barbecue. Sir, I would not have you miss it for the best horse on my plantation!"

Eventually, Kentucky would add a new wrinkle. Around Owensboro, in the western part of the state, many farmers raised sheep, and mutton became common fare at community barbecues and later in barbecue restaurants. The mutton exception distinguished Kentucky from its barbecue brethren in the rest of the region, but even there, pork became the prevailing meat. When he was doing field research for *The Kentucky Barbecue Book* (2013), Wes Berry found that barely 10 percent of the 160 restaurants he visited across the state offered mutton.

In the barbecue belt that runs from Virginia to Arkansas and includes most of the states of the old Confederacy, it's simple: Pork rules. It may be whole hog or pork shoulder, pulled or sliced, chopped or diced, or some other part like spareribs. But all of it comes from the ever-present pig.

"I have spent a good part of my life looking for the perfect barbecue," wrote Charles Kuralt, the TV journalist known for his wry "On the Road" features. "There is no point in looking in places like Texas. . . . Barbecue is pork, which narrows the search to the South, and if it's really good pork barbecue you're looking for, to North Carolina."

Kuralt, it should be noted, came from Wilmington, the place where the governor tried to sway the populace with barbecued beef.

"There are no ideas in the South," Pat Conroy once wrote, "just barbecue." The South Carolina novelist put that line in the mouth of his alter ego Tom Wingo in his best-known work, *The Prince of Tides*. The man knew how to cut to the meat of the matter.

It is hard to overstate the affection southerners have for barbecue. What the madeleine was to Proust, what chowder is to a New Englander, what pizza is to a New Yorker, barbecue is these and more to people who were raised in the land where it all began. Even if they don't eat pulled pork, the sight and smell of a roadside barbecue stand evokes primordial emotions and deep-seated memories.

In his 1987 book *Southern Food*, John Egerton, a dedicated pit follower from Kentucky, began his chapter on barbecue with a rapturous

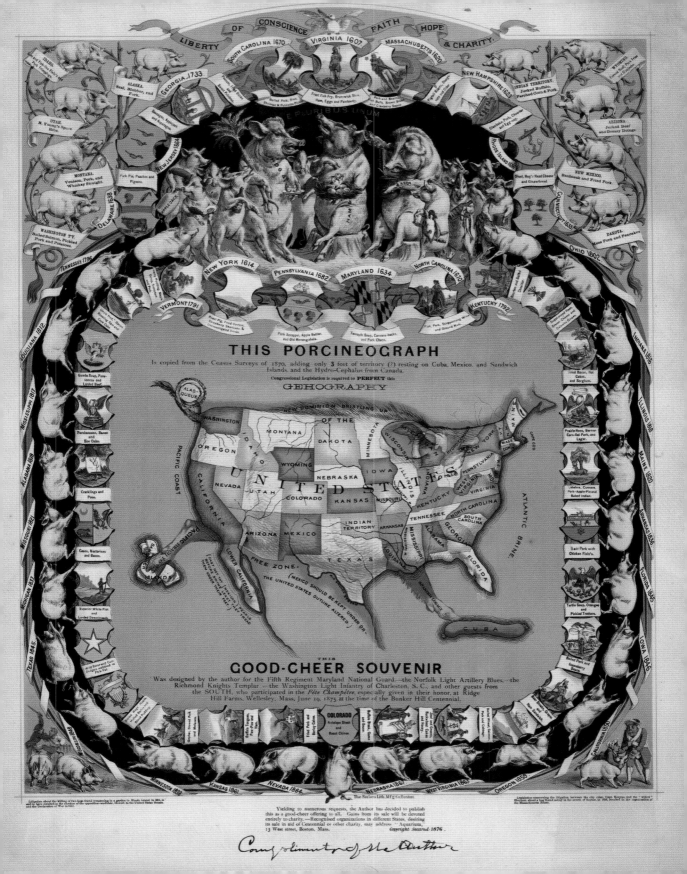

THIS PORCINEOGRAPH

Is copied from the Census Surveys of 1870, adding only **3** feet of territory (?) resting on Cuba, Mexico, and Sandwich Islands, and the Hydro-Cephalus from Canada.

Congressional Legislation is required to **PERFECT** this

GEHOGRAPY

GOOD-CHEER SOUVENIR

Was designed by the author for the Fifth Regiment Maryland National Guard,—the Norfolk Light Artillery Blues,—the Richmond Knights Templar—the Washington Light Infantry of Charleston, S. C., and other guests from the SOUTH, who participated in the *Fête Champêtre*, especially given in their honor, at Ridge Hill Farms, Wellesley, Mass., June 19, 1875, at the time of the Bunker Hill Centennial.

Yielding to numerous requests, the Author has decided to publish this as a good-cheer offering to all. Gains from its sale will be devoted entirely to charity.—Recognized organizations in different States, desiring its sale in aid of Centennial or other charity, may address "Aquarium," 13 West street, Boston, Mass. *Copyright Secured 1876.*

The Forbes Lith. Mfg. Co. Boston.

In this 1940 lithograph, the Philadelphia artist Raymond Steth fondly remembered a barbecue scene from his early childhood on a farm in North Carolina.

description of the barbecue joint of his dreams: a billow of smoke, a rack of pork, a cinder-block building painted two shades of green. "The ultimate barbecue discovery lives in the minds of countless thousands of Southerners as a seamless blend of wishful fantasy and actual experience," he wrote. "They see it shining grail-like in the distance, shimmering with all the intensity of summer heat on south Georgia asphalt: a simple shelter under a tin roof and a creosote-blackened chimney—and inside, waiting on the pit, is an utterly perfect slab of meat that has just at that very moment reached the pinnacle of readiness."

Egerton was one of the principal founders of the Southern Foodways Alliance, an academic center at the University of Mississippi that studies and celebrates the region's food and hosts an annual symposium on campus. There may be some significance in the fact that the only subject chosen as a symposium theme more than once is barbecue.

How much do southerners think about barbecue? Google Trends, which measures searches by location, calculates that eight of the top ten states originating barbecue inquiries from 2004 to 2016 were in the South, with North Carolina leading the way. The other two were border states: Kentucky (no. 7) and Missouri (no. 10).

In this era of political polarization, barbecue might be one of the few things southerners can agree on (even as they disagree on some of the particulars). When several Deep South states wrestled over removing the Confederate battle emblem from their state flags, John Shelton Reed, a sociologist at the University of North Carolina before he became a barbecue historian, suggested that the image of a dancing pig with a knife and fork would make a fitting alternative. "You want to talk about heritage, not hate," he wrote. "That represents a heritage we all share and can take pride in."

Few southerners were as prideful about barbecue as Lewis Grizzard, the Atlanta newspaper columnist who became such a successful humorist that he landed on a *Tonight Show* couch facing Johnny Carson. Journalists love to write about barbecue—look at me—but as readers of the *Atlanta Journal-Constitution* knew, it was a cradle-to-grave obsession for Grizzard.

92. A Southern Barbecue.

"A Southern Barbecue": Variations of this iconic scene appeared on postcards in the early 1900s. The author owns one that reads "A Kentucky Barbecue," postmarked 1912.

He wrote with great feeling about tasting his first sliced pork sandwich as a boy at Sprayberry's, Georgia's oldest barbecue restaurant, near his childhood home in Moreland. His mother, a schoolteacher, would order curb service and sip beer from a brown paper sack she kept on the floorboard of her '48 Chevy so no one in the small town would see her drinking. Years later, suffering from a congenital heart condition, Grizzard got a new lease on life with a transplanted valve that came (naturally) from a pig. His heart problems didn't go away. In 1994, as he awaited his fourth surgery, he wrote about some friends who brought Sprayberry's barbecue to him in the hospital. He was sick and emaciated, and it was the first thing he had enjoyed eating in days. The column was headlined: "This pig gave its life for a good cause: me."

Grizzard died two months later, at forty-seven. Sprayberry's still has on its menu a barbecue plate named for him, a memorial he would have appreciated deeply.

The Skylight Inn, the Carolina barbecue place with the Capitol dome, is one of the best spots in America to see old-time pit customs in practice. Although the restaurant opened in 1947, the owners trace their barbecue lineage deep into the 1800s, when one of their ancestors catered a Baptist gathering and saw there was money to be made from smoked pork. He started coming to town regularly to sell barbecue from a covered wagon.

Lexington, North Carolina, celebrated its barbecue heritage with a public art program called Pigs in the City. This festive porker appeared in front of the county courthouse in 2010.

"That story has been passed down through my family for generations," said Sam Jones, the great-great-great-great-grandson of that first barbecue man.

We were sitting in the dining room talking while a line of customers waited for the standard Skylight order: a cardboard tray of pork mingled with bits of crispy skin, a square of cornbread, and another tray of coleslaw on top. Behind the counter I could see James Howell, the man who for years had chopped and mixed the barbecue, whacking away with two meat cleavers. The flashing hands were mesmerizing, the rhythm infectious. It was great performance art.

Pete Jones, Sam's grandfather, founded the restaurant and came up with the idea of the Capitol dome when a writer for *National Geographic* visited in 1979. "You've come to the capital of barbecue," Pete told him, and the writer printed his quote, inspiring the curious home-improvement project on the roof.

The Skylight Inn is a throwback to the earliest days of American barbecue. They cook whole hogs over oak and hickory in a stand-alone pit building that has to be manned almost around the clock. Whole hog is the custom in eastern North Carolina, while on the other side of the state, especially around Lexington, equally esteemed barbecue places smoke only part of the pig, the pork shoulder.

"If I had to go to the barbecue festival in Lexington," Jones told me, "I probably couldn't sell enough of what I cooked to pay my hotel bill."

The James Beard Foundation was mindful of the Great Carolina Divide when it decided to honor the state's barbecue heritage in 2003. With the wisdom of Solomon, the culinary arts organization gave its America's Classics award to two restaurants simultaneously—the

Barbecue purists are reassured when they see a pile of hardwood outside a barbecue joint. This one is behind Bridges Barbecue Lodge in Shelby, North Carolina.

The Great Carolina Sauce Divide

There's been a barbecue civil war in North Carolina for more than a century, with the vinegar sauce followers in the eastern part of the state pitted against the tomato faction to the west. Here are the prototypical sauces behind the rivalry.

Pig-Pickin' Sauce

This is a standard version of America's original barbecue sauce: the tomato-less, peppery, vinegary dressing that's put on pork east of Raleigh.

Makes about 2 cups

2 cups apple cider vinegar
2 tablespoons packed brown sugar
1½ tablespoons salt (can use less)
½ tablespoon red pepper flakes
¾ teaspoon ground red pepper
1 tablespoon ground black pepper

Combine ingredients and use as a baste and sauce on barbecued pork. Stores indefinitely in a cool, dark place.

Lexington Red Splash

This is a standard version of the slightly tomatoed, peppery, vinegary sauce that North Carolinians put on barbecued pork west of Raleigh, especially around Lexington.

Makes about 2 cups

1½ cups distilled white vinegar
⅔ cup ketchup
½ cup water
1 tablespoon sugar
½ teaspoon ground black pepper
½ teaspoon ground red pepper
Pinch or two of red pepper flakes
Salt to taste

In a small saucepan, combine ingredients and simmer for 15 minutes. Use as a baste and sauce on pork. Stores indefinitely in a cool, dark place.

Skylight Inn in the east and Lexington Barbecue in the west—to avoid taking sides in the intramural rivalry.

At the time, Jones had never heard of the James Beard Foundation.

"This lady called from New York and said she wanted me to come up there and accept this award," he recalled, "and I said, 'You don't understand how tight my folks are. Ain't no way my granddaddy is going to New York on his dime to pick up some trophy.' And she said, 'Mr. Jones, you don't understand the gravity of this. This is like the Oscars of the food world.' So I told my folks about it, that this was the cat's meow of food awards, and they said, 'Well, OK, we'll pay for you to go.' First time I'd ever been to New York."

The Skylight Inn was well known among barbecue aficionados, but the award brought it much wider acclaim. Jones appeared on national TV shows and got invitations to appear at academic conferences and festivals like the Big Apple Barbecue Block Party in Manhattan. The food world seemed to embrace the restaurant as if the fundamentalist approach to barbecue that it represented was in danger of fading away.

Actually, it was.

"I think barbecue like this is probably going to die out," Jones said. "Everyone these days wants to do something quick and easy. There ain't nothing about wood-cooked barbecue that's quick and easy."

For years, barbecue places have switched from wood-fired pits to gas or to hybrid cookers that use hardwood for flavor but rely on gas or electricity to regulate the temperature. It saves on labor and fuel costs and can produce a more uniform product. Even in North Carolina, where devotion to the old ways seems strong, the number of barbecue restaurants that cook completely over wood has dwindled.

Not long after he published his Carolina barbecue book, John Shelton Reed and some friends launched the Campaign for Real Barbecue, an effort to certify and recognize authentic commercial pits that use nothing but wood. Reed, who jokes that he could have titled his book *The Sacred and the Propane*, regards barbecue restaurants that take short cuts as "gas-passers." The campaign spread to South Carolina, Kentucky, and Georgia, and got an approving write-up from Calvin Trillin in the *New Yorker*.

The Jones family epitomizes this dedication to purism. That billboard outside the restaurant that proclaims Ayden the barbecue capital of the world has another line that makes their philosophy as clear as a commandment: "If It's Not Cooked With Wood, It's Not Bar-B-Q."

Sam Jones added to the roster of true 'cue establishments in 2016 when he opened his own restaurant a few miles north of town. He cooked the same whole-hog barbecue they did at the mother

OPPOSITE: The Southern Foodways Alliance at the University of Mississippi has devoted two of its annual symposiums to barbecue, the only food afforded such attention. At the 2012 conference, participants were given trading cards honoring noted pitmasters (left to right from top): Warner Stamey of Stamey's Barbecue in Greensboro, North Carolina; Lawrence Craig of Craig's Bar-B-Q in De Valls Bluff, Arkansas; Vencil Mares of Taylor Cafe in Taylor, Texas; J. C. Hardaway of Hawkins Grill in Memphis, Tennessee; Toots Caston of Fresh Air Bar-B-Que in Jackson, Georgia; Leatha Jackson of Leatha's Bar-B-Que Inn in Hattiesburg, Mississippi; Bub Sweatman of Sweatman's Bar-B-Que in Holly Hill, South Carolina; and Big Bob Gibson of Big Bob Gibson Bar-B-Q in Decatur, Alabama.

PITMASTER
TRADING CARD SET

Southern Foodways Alliance

www.southernfoodways.org

Warner Stamey — *Stamey's Barbecue*

Lawrence Craig — *Craig's Bar-B-Q*

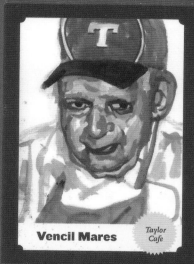

Vencil Mares — *Taylor Cafe*

J.C. Hardaway — *Hawkins Grill*

Toots Caston — *Fresh Air Bar-B-Que*

Leatha Jackson — *Leatha's Bar-B-Que Inn*

Bub Sweatman — *Sweatman's Bar-B-Que*

Big Bob Gibson — *Big Bob Gibson's Bar-B-Q*

OPPOSITE: A little
girl and a big plate of
Brunswick stew and
white bread at the May
Day pageant barbecue in
Siloam, Georgia, 1941.

ship—which he still helped run, with his father, Bruce, and his uncle Jeff—but it offered a broader menu and alcoholic beverages (which his daddy, a minister, didn't entirely approve of). The new place was called Sam Jones BBQ in homage to the old place, which no one around Ayden called the Skylight Inn. They called it Pete Jones Barbecue.

When Sam's grandfather died in 2006, among the many tributes posted on the funeral home website was one from a man in Leesburg, Virginia. "We should all thank God that Noah had the foresight to put them two hogs on the Ark so that later on Mr. Pete Jones could perfect what God created," he wrote, linking the Bible, pigs, and a Carolina barbecue place.

In the South, that all makes sense.

Mrs. Dull's Brunswick Stew

Henrietta Stanley Dull, the first food editor of the *Atlanta Journal*, was born during the Civil War and died a century later during the height of the civil rights movement. Her 1928 cookbook, *Southern Cooking*, was a standard reference for decades and included this recipe, which might seem a bit gothic for modern tastes. She's got a recipe for barbecued rabbit, too.

1 pig's head, feet, liver, and heart
4 quarts peeled and diced Irish
    potatoes
2 quarts peeled and diced tomatoes
1 quart finely cut okra
18 ears finely cut corn (or 2 cans)
2 large onions, cut fine
4 garlic buttons, tied in a cheesecloth
1 tablespoon dry mustard
Juice of 1 lemon
½ lemon, seeds removed
1 bottle Worcestershire sauce
1 medium bottle chili sauce
1 pint tomato catsup
½ pound butter
Salt, black pepper, and red pepper to
    taste
(*Note:* Sweet peppers, both green and
    red, may be used if desired.)

Thoroughly clean pig's head and feet. From the head remove the teeth and gums, upper and lower. Place head, feet, liver, and heart in boiling water and cook slowly until meat falls from bones and will come to pieces. Remove from the liquor, remove all bone and any tough part, pull to pieces and mash or chop until fine. From the liquor remove scum and replace the meat. If not much liquor, add boiling water. Add vegetables and seasonings; cook slowly and for several hours. If too thick, add hot water; if thin, add light bread crumbs, one large loaf.

When ready to serve, add butter. Stir almost constantly during the cooking. If it should stick or scorch, change the vessel, as any scorch will ruin the entire stew.

Barbecue Pits, Fairgrounds, Oklahoma City, Okla.

3

Big Feeds

The greatest barbecue in American history was staged for a less-than-great leader.

On January 9, 1923, John Calloway "Jack" Walton was sworn in as the fifth governor of the young state of Oklahoma. A populist Democrat, he wanted an inaugural celebration that invoked the memory of Andrew Jackson's when he became president almost a century before and opened the White House to a crowd of people who got rowdy on spiked punch. Walton planned a parade, square dance, and barbecue for as many people as Oklahoma City could handle. In the weeks leading up the event, it became clear that was going to be a lot of people.

Thousands of carpenters started building the barbecue infrastructure at the state fairgrounds on New Year's Day, constructing tables and chairs, platforms, and temporary dining facilities. Workers dug six trenches running a quarter mile each and filled them with nineteen railroad cars of wood. Two days out, the pits were ignited and the cooking commenced. Armies of livestock, game, and poultry were laid over the coals: 289 head of cattle, 70 hogs, 36 sheep, 2,000 pounds of buffalo, 1,500 pounds of reindeer, 2,540 rabbits, 134 possums, 25 squirrels, 1,427 chickens, 210 turkeys, 34 ducks, 14 geese, 15 deer, and one lonely antelope.

Inauguration Day began with a parade that stretched more than ten miles and included one hundred bands, cowboys and Indians on horseback, and floats from each of Oklahoma's counties. At its conclusion, Walton took the oath of office in front of the throng—it was a reenactment; he had actually taken it the night before at the state

OPPOSITE: The inauguration of Jack Walton as Oklahoma governor in 1923 might have been the biggest feed in the annals of American barbecue. The great feast drew national attention and was the occasion for souvenir postcards like this one.

capitol—and only then were people allowed to partake of the feast they had been smelling for hours. All afternoon and evening, thousands filed through fifteen serving sheds to get piles of meat, bread, and pickles, some of them going back for seconds, until an estimated 125,000 meals had been dispensed.

"It was a big day, a big time—and it was the biggest barbecue," the *Daily Oklahoman* concluded, predicting that it would receive worldwide attention.

Journals far and wide did carry news of the extravaganza. The *New York Times* published several dispatches. Souvenir postcards were issued.

But then, like a delayed burp, the governor was expelled—impeached and removed from office before the end of the year for corruption and abuse of power and for having the brass to take on the Ku Klux Klan, which was frighteningly influential then. Jack Walton was remembered as a man who didn't know how to navigate state government but certainly knew how to throw a party. As Dan Lackey, the head of the barbecue committee, put it: "Man, wasn't that the barbecue of all barbecues?"

When we speak of barbecue today, we usually mean something served at a restaurant or cooked on a backyard grill or smoker. The word meant neither of those things for much of our history. Well into the twentieth century, "barbecue" usually referred to an event—a political meeting, a church dinner, a community gathering—where barbecued meats were the centerpiece of the festivities. It was an occasion first, a food second.

Political barbecues were already a staple of colonial life before the Revolution. Playwright Robert Munford mentions one in *The Candidates; or, The Humours of a Virginia Election*, a 1770 satire about a contest for a seat in the House of Burgesses. It's considered one of the first comedies written in America.

George Washington, as we've seen, made note in his diary of social barbecues he attended, and later presided over the ox roast at the laying of the cornerstone for the U.S. Capitol. He was not, however, the president who sealed the association of barbecue and politics in the new republic. That was the seventh chief executive, Andrew Jackson of Tennessee, who held the first barbecue at the White House in 1829. His nickname, Old Hickory, had to do with his toughness as a military leader, not his choice of hardwoods for cooking.

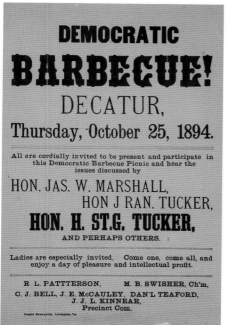

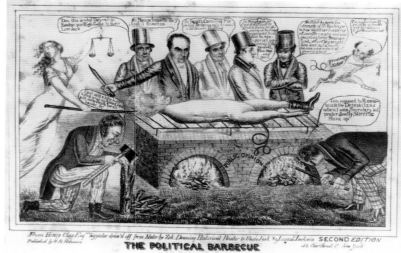

THE POLITICAL BARBECUE

In an 1834 editorial cartoon, President Andrew Jackson
was roasted like a pig.

Poster for a political barbecue in Virginia, 1894.

During the Jacksonian era, competing factions evolved into political parties, and candidates openly campaigned for office at rallies,
bonfires, and barbecues. Jackson's Democratic Party was especially
fond of barbecues. During the election of 1832, the *Louisville Journal*,
a Whig newspaper in Kentucky, pilloried the opposition for its love
of pork and liquor: "They have one sort of answering for everything.
If we show them that we have elected our Lieutenant Governor by a
majority of nearly 30,000, *they reply by swallowing a pig*. If we show
them that we have gained great strength in the Senate, and added
to our superiority, *they reply by devouring a turkey*. If we show
them that we have attained a majority of two-thirds in the House of
Representatives, *they reply by pouring off a pint of whiskey or apple-
toddy*. There is no withstanding such arguments. We give it up."

Jackson himself was the butt of a memorable 1834 editorial cartoon captioned "The Political Barbecue." It shows the president
roasting on a bed of coals labeled "Public Opinion," one of his boots
removed to reveal a cloven pig's foot, as his enemies hover over him—
one of them, Daniel Webster, brandishing a butcher's knife.

The Whigs used barbecues to their own ends in the presidential
election of 1840. They wanted to portray their nominee, William

Henry Harrison, as a man of the people even though he came from a plantation manor in Virginia. His campaign staged enormous barbecues and displayed log cabins to symbolize his supposedly humble roots. While the image makeover worked—Harrison won—some voters disapproved of what the barbecue hoopla implied about the values of the electorate. "There is not much difficulty in the South in raising money for a barbecue, or to buy whiskey for political purposes," wrote the Reverend J. D. Long, an abolitionist minister in Philadelphia, "but when the funds are wanted for a library, that is quite another question."

Political barbecues were by no means limited to the West or the South. During the 1860 election, backers of Stephen A. Douglas held an ox roast in New York City for the nominee of the Northern Democrats. The humor weekly *Vanity Fair* made sport of the occasion in a parody of a Walt Whitman poem it called "The Song of the Barbecue." A typical stanza:

> Jerk it off from the sirloin, rump,
> Ribs or shoulder, haunch or quarter,
> Throw it to the starving crowd,
> Bloody, half-cooked though it may be
> Each Bite is a Bite for Douglas!

Frank Leslie's Illustrated Weekly ran a lively scene of an 1871 ox barbecue in New York City.

Douglas fell a few bites short in the election that fall, losing to Abraham Lincoln, who had a long history with barbecue himself. It started before he was born when his parents, Nancy Hanks and Thomas Lincoln, celebrated their 1806 wedding in Kentucky with a barbecue that included bear, venison, and wild turkey. Their son launched his political career in Illinois during the heyday of campaign barbecues and honed his folksy speaking style at countless such gatherings. During the U.S. Senate campaign of 1858, Lincoln was the guest of honor at a barbecue in Urbana and, according to one witness, insisted that a server take his place at the head of the table while he sat on the ground gnawing on a turkey leg and a biscuit.

Barbecues were such an enshrined part of politics during the nineteenth century that the grounds of the U.S. Capitol had two spaces set aside for parties to hold rallies over smoked meats. The landscape architect Frederick Law Olmsted noted the "barbecue groves" when he was commissioned in 1874 to develop a new plan for the property. He reported that a dozen trees had been planted on the east side of the Capitol during the Jackson administration, forming two areas, "one probably intended for Democrat, the other for Whig jollifications."

But politics was far from the only reason for such "jollifications."

Barbecues were one of the most common forms of public entertainment during the 1800s and early 1900s and were organized for almost any occasion, great or small.

There were barbecues for war. When southern states seceded from the Union, communities across the region sent their soldiers off with a parade and a pig roast, carrying on a tradition of militia barbecues going back to the 1700s.

There were barbecues for peace. For decades after the Civil War, veterans on both sides reassembled for reunion barbecues. One of the largest barbecues in American history, serving one hundred thousand, was for the 1895 meeting of the Grand Army of the Republic in Louisville, Kentucky. Sometimes the former enemies met at reconciliation gatherings like the one in 1889 that drew 25,000 of the blue and gray to Chickamauga, Georgia, the site of one of the bloodiest battles of the war. "The barbecue was specifically prepared and tendered by the ex-Confederates to the Union soldiers," reported the *Washington Post*.

There were barbecues for freedom. The formerly enslaved people of the South frequently celebrated Emancipation Day with barbecues—which was only fitting since they had usually cooked the food at plantation barbecues before the war. The observances took on a special character in Texas, where the Emancipation Proclamation was virtually unknown until the state's military governor announced it on June 19, 1865. Juneteenth, as the anniversary was known, became a traditional day for black Texans to gather at picnics and barbecues to remember.

Thousands of Union and Confederate veterans gathered in 1889 for a reconciliation barbecue on the Chickamauga battlefield in Georgia. Participants received this invitation and a pipe of peace.

There were barbecues opposed to that freedom. The Ku Klux Klan, renowned for its love of bonfires and flaming crosses, used barbecue as a recruiting tool all over the country—not just in the South—especially during its rebirth in the 1920s. The Klan ran newspaper ads and printed posters for a homecoming in Evansville, Indiana, that touted "BRASS BANDS . . . A BIG BARBECUE . . . ONE DAZZLING DAY OF DIVERSIFIED DELIGHTS!"

A stereopticon view of the barbecue pits at the 1895 encampment of the Grand Army of the Republic in Louisville, Kentucky.

GRAND BARBECUE
OF THE
WALKER COLORED VOTERS!!
OF
RICHMOND AND HENRICO.

We, a portion of the Walker Colored Voters of Richmond City and Henrico County, intend giving a Barbecue to our Colored Political friends, on

FRIDAY AFTERNOON, AT 3 O'CLOCK, JULY 2,
ON VAUXALL ISLAND, MAYO'S BRIDGE.

Every colored voter in favor of the equal political and civil rights of the colored and white man; who is in favor of expurgating from the Constitution the Test Oath and the Disfranchising Clause; who is in favor of the adoption of the Constitution when amended; who favors the election of the **WALKER TICKET**, and desires a sincere, lasting peace between the White and the Colored race, is earnestly invited to attend and participate. Good speakers, white and colored, will address the meeting. The committee of arrangements will take all necessary measures to insure good order and the comfort of the guests.

COMMITTEE OF ARRANGEMENTS.

Lomax B Smith, Chm'n	Jas H Clark	Elmore Brown
R C Hobson	George Keys	Wm Thornton
Jno H Cooley	John Scott	Albert Cook
Joseph Louis	Jas Hopes	Moses Rison
F C H Cole	Isaac H Hunter	Patrick Jackson
John Clark	Robt P Bolling	John West
Abram Hall	Wm Bradley	John Jackson

LIST OF SUBSCRIBERS.

Elmore Brown, John Jackson, Pat Jackson, R C Hobson, Jas Bundy, Moses Rison, Albert Cook, John West, R Roney, Stephen Jones, Warner Allen, James Winnie, Frederick Burger, Theodore Hopes, Wm Young, E Walker, James Hopes, B Randolph, E Froman, Jas H Clark, John Clark, Saml Booker, Fleming Mitchell, Robt P Bolling, John Johnson, Joseph Louis, Abram Hall, Wm Bradley, Frederick C Cole, J B Mason, Theodore Scott, Thos Griffin, Robt Hamilton, Dorson Gardner, George Page, George Keys, Henry Washington, G W Hughes, Horace Johnson, Andrew Johnson, Jeff Sheppard, Jack Watkins, Richard Chiles, Daniel Davis, Joseph Walker, Henry Chamberlain, Stephen Nicholas, Frank Hancock, John H Smith, John Cowley, John J Scott, John W. Cooley, Jesse Bailey, Stephen Nelson, Cornelius Parrot, Edward Hill, Jas Hill, Jos Hill, Edward Stevens, Frank Hill, John Watkins, James Chester, Thos Bean, Chas Taliaferro, Wm Taylor, John Cooper, Richard Meekins, Sam Patch, Benj Coots, Wm Chelser, Wm Coots, Wallace Jones, Frank Backman, Hamilton Johnson, R Harris, Jas Butler, Wm Mitchell, Coleman Tinsley, Ed Henderson, Stephen Sett, James Traylor, Wm Hayes, John Butler, Frank Johnson, James Johnson, Benj Chester, Isaac H. Hunter, Henry Anderson, James Mitchell, Wm. Lee, S Mitchell, A Watkins, Nelson Davis, John Davis, and 200 others.

[handwritten] Copy by Moses Rison
July 1, 1869

Shriners barbecue in Silver Spring, Maryland, 1922.

There were barbecues for good causes, like churches and schools and better transportation. During the 1800s, railroad companies promoted the construction of new lines by throwing barbecues meant to entice potential investors. Towns celebrated with barbecues when they received new rail service, as San Angelo, Texas, did in 1888 when the Santa Fe line started bringing passengers. Years later, when automobiles came, communities used barbecues to drum up support for improved highways. "Good Roads Barbecue," read a 1919 headline in the *Atlanta Constitution* when the town of East Point marked the completion of a paved two-lane to the state capital. Other stories in Atlanta announced barbecues for new bridges and even parking garages.

There were fraternal barbecues for the Elks and the Odd Fellows and the Shriners and the Knights of Pythias. There were company barbecues for textile mills and brick factories and coal mines and furniture manufacturers. There were employee barbecues for clerks and schoolteachers and police officers and assembly line workers. There were convention barbecues for bankers and electricians and insurance men and funeral directors.

There were barbecues for sinners and for those who preached against sin. During the summer of 1913, Baptist ministers held a barbecue in Atlanta followed a month later by one for the bartenders union.

There were barbecues for the highest stations of life and for the lowest. Music lovers in Atlanta threw a barbecue in 1915 for visiting stars from the Metropolitan Opera. During the same period, the poor people in the county almshouse and the convict camp enjoyed their annual barbecues.

There were barbecues that went terribly wrong. At the National Western Stock Show in Denver, a free barbecue advertised to the public in 1898 descended into chaos when thirty thousand people rushed the Union Pacific stockyards and made off with much of the meat, beer, and utensils. "The game fields of the West were ransacked to secure material for a menu such as kings might rejoice at," the *Rocky Mountain News* observed, "and the result [was] turned over to be fought for by hoodlums."

Finally, there were barbecues that simply defy description. In 1898, deep in the heart of Texas, the *Austin American-Statesman* took note of one with this headline:

"Big BBQ at Lunatic Asylum."

Everyone, it seems, wanted a barbecue.

Kentucky Burgoo

Talk about big feeds. *The Southern Cook Book of Fine Old Recipes*, a 1939 volume in which this appeared, says the recipe makes 1,200 gallons. It comes from "a handwritten copy by Mr. J. T. Looney of Lexington . . . Kentucky's most famous Burgoo-maker," for whom Burgoo King, the winner of the 1932 Kentucky Derby, was named. Read to the end; you don't see many recipes using that last ingredient anymore.

600 pounds lean soup meat (no fat, no bones)
200 pounds fat hens
2,000 pounds potatoes, peeled and diced
200 pounds onions
5 bushels cabbage, chopped
60 (10-pound) cans of tomatoes
24 (10-pound) cans of pureed tomatoes
24 (10-pound) cans of carrots
18 (10-pound) cans of corn
Red pepper and salt to taste
Worcestershire, Tabasco, or A.1. sauce to taste

Mix the ingredients a little at a time and cook outside in huge iron kettles over wood fires for 15 to 20 hours. Use squirrels in season . . . one dozen squirrels to each 100 gallons.

Snake hunt and barbecue in Chadwick, Missouri, 1969.

Ad for a lamb slaying and barbecue cruise in the *Washington Bee*, 1895.

Soldiers at a war bond barbecue in Atlanta, 1945.

In 1942, at the beginning of World War II, Dorothea Lange photographed a barbecue among Japanese Americans in California awaiting removal to internment camps.

Jack Walton's inauguration in Oklahoma set off a wave of gargantuan gubernatorial barbecues. In Louisiana, Governor Sam Houston Jones took office in 1940 at a barbecue so large it had to be held in the LSU football stadium. A year later in Texas, Pappy O'Daniel had a trench dug in the lawn of the governor's mansion to smoke thousands of pounds of beef for twenty-five thousand people at his inauguration.

If anything, the political barbecue became an even bigger institution by the middle of the twentieth century. Voters, especially in the South and Southwest, came to expect free meat (not to mention whiskey) with their stump speeches. Sometimes politics overtook barbecues founded for other purposes. The Fancy Farm Picnic, in the bucolic town of that name in western Kentucky, started in 1880 as a Catholic fund-raiser but is known today as a place for candidates and constituents to mingle over pork and mutton. The Mallard Creek Presbyterian Church Barbecue in Charlotte, North Carolina, began in 1929 as a way to pass the hat and pay off a building debt. It soon became one of the don't-miss dates on the Tar Heel political calendar. "No man has been

A staffer enjoying barbecue at the inauguration of Florida governor Fuller Warren, 1949.

The Oak Grove United Methodist Church barbecue in Decatur, Georgia, is one of the largest in the Deep South.

A vintage ad for the Mallard Creek Presbyterian Church barbecue in Charlotte, North Carolina, one of the biggest in the country.

BARBECUED *WHAT?*

One of the oddest political barbecues ever held honored the largest man ever to be president. William Howard Taft spent six weeks before his 1909 inauguration at a luxury resort in Augusta, Georgia. With the president-elect so close by, the Atlanta Chamber of Commerce seized the opportunity to promote the city and invited him to a banquet. The main dish: Barbecued Opossum with Persimmon Sauce.

The choice of entree wasn't as strange as it seems. Americans ate a wider range of meats then, and possum was not yet a roadkill joke, especially in the South. There was some political silliness at work as well. Taft's predecessor, Theodore Roosevelt, had become identified with the Teddy Bear after a hunting trip in Mississippi. The popular imagination demanded a similar mascot for Taft, and editorial cartoonists settled on a portly critter named Billy Possum. The Atlantans decided to cook one for the incoming president.

For days, newspapers ran features about the search for the tastiest marsupial in Georgia. At the banquet on January 15, six hundred guests filled the floor of the Municipal Auditorium and watched as a waiter ferried the unfortunate selection in a chafing dish down the middle aisle and presented it to the guest of honor. He lifted the lid and, in the words of the *Atlanta Journal*, the main course "sat grinning in a bed of gravy and sweet potatoes."

Taft, an Ohio native who had never tried possum, took an exploratory nibble, smiled, then dug in and pronounced himself pleased. But he soon tired of Billy Possum. When admirers in Cairo, Illinois, presented him a live specimen as a gift, he thanked them but admitted that he didn't really "hanker for it."

The *New York Times* seemed puzzled by the whole affair. While its story about the Atlanta banquet made the front page—headline: "Taft Eats 'Possum"—an editorialist considered such victuals beneath the dignity of the office: "It is not part of the President's duty to eat strange foods merely to satisfy neighborhood pride. We earnestly beg Mr. Taft to stop with the 'possum."

We love "BILLY POSSUM"
his coat is so warm
If even we EAT him
he'll do us no harm;
No more Teddy Bear
will we fondle with glee,
Billy Possum in future
our "Mascot" shall be.

A souvenir postcard for Billy Possum, the short-lived mascot of President William Howard Taft, who bravely sampled the barbecue meat Atlantans put before him.

Barbecued chicken under the Spanish moss in Kissimmee, Florida, 1955.

elected governor of North Carolina without eating more barbecue than was good for him," Raleigh newspaperman Herbert O'Keefe wrote in the 1950s, and the same was true of other states.

While most politicians used barbecue to rally supporters and raise money, one used it as a metaphor. In a 1935 radio address, Senator Huey Long of Louisiana pitched his wealth-redistribution ideas as a simple matter of mealtime fairness: "I wonder if any of you people who are listening to me were ever at a barbecue. We used to go there—sometimes 1,000 people or more. If there were 1,000 people, we would put enough meat and bread and everything else on the table for 1,000 people. Then everybody would be called and everyone would eat all they wanted. But suppose at one of these barbecues for 1,000 people that one man took 90 percent of the food and ran off with it and ate until he got sick and let the balance rot. . . . Well, ladies and gentlemen, America—all the people of America—have been invited to a barbecue. God invited us all to come and eat and drink all we wanted."

If there was one name that became synonymous with political barbecues, it was the Talmadges of Georgia. Their run started in the 1920s with Eugene Talmadge, a rural populist who would stand on

SPACE COWBOYS

As the United States geared up to put a man on the moon, the federal government decided to build a space flight center in Texas. On July 4, 1962, Houstonians welcomed NASA and the Mercury astronauts to town with one of the damnedest barbecues ever thrown.

John Glenn, Alan Shepard, and the others were spirited through the sweltering city in a parade led by the cowboy-hat-waving congressman who had helped bring home the brisket, Representative Albert H. Thomas. The procession led to the civic coliseum, where, as Tom Wolfe described the scene in *The Right Stuff*: "The air was filled with the stench of burning cattle. They had set up about ten barbecue pits in there, and they were roasting thirty animals. Five thousand businessmen and politicians and their better halves, fresh from the 100-degree horrors of Downtown in July, couldn't wait to sink their faces in it. It was a Texas barbecue, Houston-style."

The astronauts and their families were seated in folding chairs on the arena floor, surrounded by a security ring of Texas Rangers, as thousands of people in the stands intently watched them eat. It was one of the earliest examples of barbecue as a spectator sport.

Twenty-seven years later, in 1989, NASA actually sent barbecue into orbit with the space shuttle *Discovery*. Astronaut Sonny Carter requested a meal from one of his favorite hometown restaurants, Fincher's, in Macon, Georgia, so Mission Control found itself freeze-drying, not Texas beef, but Georgia pork. Fincher's still displays a tray of the stuff at its flagship location, along with a framed certificate from NASA.

John and Annie Glenn at the 1962 barbecue Houston threw to welcome NASA to town.

the podium snapping his red suspenders, a flock of hair flying loose, and tear into the city slickers in the state capitol and "them lyin' Atlanta newspapers" that told on him. He liked to say that there were only three things that the poor dirt farmers of Georgia could trust: God almighty, the Sears Roebuck catalog, and Gene Talmadge.

Ole Gene, as he was known, kicked off his 1932 campaign for governor with a barbecue that drew ten thousand people to McRae, his hometown in the piney woods of middle Georgia. Farmers donated scores of pigs, cows, goats, and chickens, and a local man nicknamed the Barbecue King, Norman Graham, oversaw the cooking. A crowd of townspeople came out to watch the preparations, suggesting that the ritual of the barbecue was as much an attraction as the speechifying. In his Talmadge biography, *The Wild Man from Sugar Creek*, William Anderson described the eve of the barbecue:

> Some were so enthralled by the enormity of the scene that they stayed long into the night, close by the dull glow of the coals to stare into the fires the Barbecue King had built and to be able to say, "I was there."

THE SADDEST BARBECUES

Two of the darkest days in American history involved barbecues that never happened.

Franklin D. Roosevelt sent word that he would attend a barbecue hosted by the mayor of Warm Springs, Georgia, on April 12, 1945. The president said he'd pass on the pork but would like some Brunswick stew and an Old Fashioned cocktail. FDR had visited Warm Springs dozens of times since he was stricken with polio in 1921 and enjoyed picnics atop a nearby mountain, Dowdell's Knob, where his party would cook out on a stone barbecue pit. He didn't make this barbecue; he died of a cerebral hemorrhage that afternoon.

Lyndon B. Johnson planned a big barbecue at his ranch outside Austin when President John F. Kennedy visited Texas for a political trip on November 22, 1963. The staff was making final preparations when the shocking news came that Kennedy had been killed in Dallas. As president, Johnson hosted scores of barbecues at the LBJ Ranch. The first was barely a month after the assassination, for the chancellor of West Germany. The *New York Herald-Tribune* called it "barbecue diplomacy."

Jimmy and Billy Carter eating barbecue in Billy's gas station in Plains, Georgia, during the 1976 presidential campaign.

Insects swirled and buzzed crazily out of the night, whizzing around and crashing into the string of naked light bulbs that wound over the pits giving a hard brightness to the cooking area. So many bugs wandered into the kettle of stew, drawn there by its sweet aroma, that no pepper had to be added for flavor.

As one of the men explained, "Bugs was good spice."

After Gene died, his son, Herman Talmadge, followed him as governor and continued the barbecue tradition. He and his wife, Betty, lived in a white-columned house near Atlanta that was said to be a model for the Twelve Oaks plantation in *Gone with the Wind*, the site of a famous fictional barbecue. Betty Talmadge took that heritage to heart and staged barbecue galas at the house for conventioneers, special parties, and latter-day politicians like Jimmy Carter when he ran for president. She wrote a book about her career as a southern hostess in 1977, calling it *How to Cook a Pig*.

By then, the role of political barbecues was evolving. They were still used to raise money or celebrate victories or thank supporters, but they weren't regular stops on the campaign trail anymore. With the spread of mass media, there were better ways to connect with voters than a big feed.

Marvin Griffin, a former Georgia governor, learned about the changing times when he tried to regain the office in 1962. He ran an old-fashioned campaign, crisscrossing the state and drawing large, raucous crowds with the lure of fiery rhetoric and free barbecue. His opponent, Carl Sanders, a handsome young attorney and exemplar of New South leadership, concentrated on broadcast advertising and skipped the barbecue circuit. He won in a landslide.

After the election, Griffin admitted that he might have relied on an outmoded strategy, putting it in colorful terms that Gene Talmadge would have appreciated. "Everybody that ate my barbecue," he said, "I don't believe voted for me."

He was being humorous, in a rueful way, but he was also pronouncing an elegy for a fading era.

Reprints of this oil painting, suitable for framing without advertising, will be sent upon request. Write United States Brewers Foundation, 21 East 40th Street, New York City.

Western Barbecue by FLETCHER MARTIN

One of a series of typical American scenes and customs painted by America's foremost artists

A barbecue on one of our great western ranches, clambakes on New England's beaches, ball games on a sand lot or in a big-league stadium . . . all these are America, the land we love, the land that today we fight for.

In this America of tolerance and good humor, of neighborliness and pleasant living, perhaps no beverage more fittingly belongs than wholesome, friendly beer. And the right to enjoy this beverage of moderation . . . this, too, is part of our own American heritage of personal freedom.

AMERICA'S BEVERAGE OF MODERATION

Beer belongs . . . enjoy it

"MORALE IS A LOT OF LITTLE THINGS"
•••V MAIL
MAIL THAT LETTER TODAY

4

South by Southwest

There are scores of hotels and restaurants on the National Register of Historic Places, but as far as I can tell, no barbecue joint has ever made the roll of honor. Most barbecue people would rather turn meat than worry about a brass plaque. Still, it does seem an omission when you consider how essentially American the food is and how vintage and storied some of the places that serve it are.

If any barbecue property deserved to be first on the register, it would be the two-story brick building at 208 South Commerce Street in Lockhart, Texas: Smitty's Market. Smitty's is a barbecue place that used to be the home of Kreuz Market, founded in 1900 by a German American who was typical of the central Europeans who brought smoked sausage to Texas. Charles Kreuz (rhymes with "bites") ran a butcher shop and grocery and sold a little barbecue on the side. As the collateral business grew, the market moved into its current space in 1924 and started using what might be the nation's oldest barbecue pit in continuous operation. It's one of the highlights of any Texas barbecue pilgrimage.

Entering the restaurant from the street, you walk down a long, dim hallway whose walls seem varnished by decades of smoke. At the end, you feel heat rising from one side of the ordering counter. Getting closer, you see what appears to be a roaring campfire right there on the floor; it looks like something a caveman, or at least a cowboy, would cook over. If you enter from the back, from the parking lot, you can pass close enough to the blaze to toast marshmallows. The pile of crackling post oak feeds an L-shaped brick pit covered by heavy metal lids raised by a pulley system. A chimney rises thirty-five feet

OPPOSITE:
A romanticized view of western barbecue appeared in a 1945 magazine ad taken out by the brewing industry, part of a series extolling American culture.

from the corner, creating a draft strong enough to pull smoke from the open fire over grates loaded with blackened beef shoulder.

Smitty's looks like no other barbecue place in America. It's hard to imagine a building inspector allowing such a cooking setup today. "The insurance company came in and told us that we needed to put a rail around that fire," said Jim Sells, who married into the family that bought the establishment from Kreuz's sons in 1948. "We told them that if you put a rail around it, the first thing that's going to happen is someone's going to touch the rail and get burned."

In all these decades, he deadpanned, "nobody has ever fallen into that fire."

And there still isn't a rail around it. In Texas, some things are too sacred to change.

Jim Sells checks the ancient pit at Smitty's Market in Lockhart, Texas.

Texas Barbecue Beans

Vencil Mares opened the Taylor Cafe in Taylor, Texas, in 1948, serving barbecue for decades at what was essentially a small-town honky-tonk. In 2002 he contributed the recipe for one of his favorite side dishes to Robb Walsh's *Legends of Texas Barbecue Cookbook.*

Makes about 6 cups

1 pound dried pinto beans
½ onion, finely chopped
1 tablespoon chili powder
1 teaspoon ground black pepper
1 cup finely chopped bacon
Salt to taste

Sort the beans to remove any stone or grit. Rinse in a colander and place the beans in a crockpot with 6 cups of water. Add the other ingredients and cook on high for 2 hours. Turn to low and allow to simmer for 8 hours, or overnight. Add more water as needed.

Robb Walsh, the Houston food writer who has chronicled Texas barbecue longer than just about anyone, once described the pit culture of the Lone Star State with a comparison: "Southern barbecue is a proud thoroughbred whose bloodlines are easily traced. Texas barbecue is a feisty mutt with a whole lot of crazy relatives."

I'm not sure southern barbecue is quite that thoroughbred—we've got a few sheep and wild boars in our bloodlines—but I get his drift. Texas is the place where the South and the Southwest meet, where the Dixie Pig mingles with Mexico, with cowboys and longhorns and Old World butcher shops, to make something at once singular and multifaceted. Like Texas itself.

Texas Monthly magazine tried to distill the complexities of the state's barbecue in 1973, just as people were beginning to consider it worth studying. "At first blush, the East Texas chopped pork sandwich with hot sauce has little in common with the slab of central Texas beef. Culturally and historically they are miles apart. It seems likely that they are the product of two quite different traditions, one carried eastward from the open range, the other carried westward by Southern blacks."

That second part gets overshadowed sometimes. Walsh has a theory about it. As memories of the Civil War receded, he believes, Texans wanted to downplay their connections to slavery and the

Confederacy and emphasize the western aspect of their history; they wanted to think of themselves as the descendants of cowboys and Rangers, not planters and cotton pickers. That led to a widespread assumption that Texas barbecue developed from the campfires of cattle country, with an assist from those Germans and Czechs who immigrated to the central part of the state and, like Kreuz, opened meat markets. According to a charming creation story that gets repeated from time to time, the word "barbecue" originated from a cattle brand that said Bar-BQ—not very likely since easterners had been holding barbecues for more than a hundred years by the time Anglos started branding steers in Texas during the early 1800s.

As elsewhere in North America, the earliest cooking that resembled barbecue in Texas was done by native tribes. Then came the Spanish and Mexican shepherds and vaqueros who tended livestock and cooked over open fires. And then came American settlers, many of them from Tennessee and Kentucky, who brought their southern barbecue ways.

Sam Houston, who led the army that won independence from Mexico at the Battle of San Jacinto in 1836, was one of them. Born in Virginia, he rose to eminence in Tennessee, where he was elected governor, and went on to become the first president of the Republic of Texas. Newspaper accounts from the 1840s show that the great man was honored with barbecues in Crockett, Texas, *and* Nashville, Tennessee.

Like many of the southerners who migrated west, Houston owned slaves. They and their progeny put their stamp on Texas barbecue, especially in the eastern part of the state, where they barbecued cattle and pigs at religious camp meetings and Emancipation celebrations, and opened some of the earliest barbecue stands in Houston, Beaumont, and other cities.

One legendary barbecue place managed to weave all those threads together in Huntsville, Texas (coincidentally, where Sam Houston is buried). The New Zion Missionary Baptist Church Barbecue began in 1979 when member Annie Mae Ward cooked for a crew that was painting the church. Everyone liked her barbecue so much that they decided to keep the pit burning to raise funds and built a ramshackle structure next to the sanctuary to use as a restaurant. It became a much-photographed scene of roadside Americana off the interstate between Houston and Dallas, as beloved for its rustic look as for its pork ribs and chopped beef sandwich.

New Zion Missionary
Baptist Church Barbecue,
Huntsville, Texas, 2007.

Some members called it the Church of the Holy Smoke. The pastor's business cards said, simply, "CHURCH BBQ: America's Food."

In the 1960 John Wayne movie *The Alamo*, there's a scene that alludes to one of the greatest truisms about Texas barbecue. Davy Crockett and the men holed up in the mission are getting sick of eating salt pork and decide to make a daring run behind Mexican lines to rustle some cattle. Afterward, chewing on beef ribs, one of the buckskinned volunteers says, "Hog never could rightly pass for meat—but beef . . ."

The idea that Texans disdain pork barbecue isn't quite right. Of the three specialties that make up the holy trinity of Texas barbecue—brisket, smoked sausage, and ribs—two of them involve creatures that oink: the sausage (which often includes pork) and the ribs (all in). Pork is common in East Texas barbecue and shows up regularly in other parts of the state that are less culturally southern. At Cooper's Old Time Pit Bar-B-Que in Llano, northwest of Austin, one of the state's top-rated places, they smoke everything from beef to goat to turkeys, but they bill themselves as "the home of The Big Chop," a two-inch-thick pork chop.

So Texas barbecue isn't exactly anti-pork, but it's clearly pro-beef, as you would expect in a state where cattle figure so prominently

Several Texas barbecue places, including House Park in Austin, claim their brisket is so tender it doesn't require a full set of choppers.

in lore and trade. And the king of all cuts is undoubtedly the sinewy, hardworking tandem of muscles across the cow's upper chest—the *pectoralis profundus* and *pectoralis superficialis*—otherwise known as brisket.

The embrace of brisket is a relatively recent phenomenon. Until the 1960s, most beef was shipped in sides—half the steer—and few people asked specifically for a brisket. While some barbecue places smoked it, brisket was usually the province of Jewish delis (and remains a favorite dish in Jewish home cooking, where it's roasted in an oven). Only after the beef industry adopted more uniform cuts did the boneless brisket we know today become universally associated with Texas barbecue.

The career of Walter Jetton, the king of the cowboy barbecuers, illustrates the transition from sides to brisket.

Walter Jetton, a Fort Worth caterer (standing under the first *b* in "barbecue," found fame as Lyndon B. Johnson's barbecue man.

Already well known because of his Fort Worth restaurant and catering business, Jetton gained a national audience during the 1960s as Lyndon B. Johnson's favorite pit boss. He staged most of the public barbecues at the LBJ Ranch and cooked for the Mexican president, the German chancellor, and several other heads of state. He turned his experiences into a book, *Walter Jetton's LBJ Barbecue Cookbook* (1965), and was named chairman of National Barbecue Month.

Jetton was a portly fellow who wore horn-rim glasses, but when he catered an event, he donned a white Stetson and string tie and became a culinary cowboy. He even called his delivery vans chuckwagons. He liked to cook sides of beef directly over a trench of hardwood embers, as they did in olden days, and sometimes disparaged conveniences like brick pits and portable cookers. As a national spokesman for barbecue, however, he accommodated himself to modern times and advised suburban cooks to buy brisket and use wood chunks to get smoke flavor on their charcoal grills.

One video from the 1960s shows him demonstrating a playful trick. "If a fire flames up," he says, "here's a water pistol to put it out and add to the Wild West atmosphere."

He squirts at the flames, grinning for all the backyard buckaroos out there.

When people think about Texas barbecue, they usually think about the center cut of the state, the region settled by Germans and Czechs during the 1800s, an area within a ninety-minute drive of Austin that includes San Antonio, the Hill Country, and the small towns where some of the most revered barbecue joints are located.

Places like LaGrange, where a Prussian family opened the Prause Meat Market in 1904 and their descendants were still serving barbecue more than a century later. Or Elgin, home of Southside Market & Barbeque, where they started smoking a spicy sausage known as Texas "hot guts" during the 1880s. Or Taylor, where Vencil Mares came back from service as an army medic during the Allied invasion of Europe and learned barbecue at Southside, leaving to start the Taylor Cafe in 1948. Some seventy years later, the modest establishment still looks like it did then, down to the dual doors that once allowed whites and Mexicans to enter on one side of the bar and blacks on the other.

A few blocks away in Taylor is Louie Mueller Barbecue, one of the most famous smoked meat emporiums in Texas, founded by a grocer

Butchers outside the J. R. Machu grocery in Granger, Texas, 1903. Machu's was typical of the meat markets that brought central European sausage to Lone Star barbecue.

of German extraction in 1949. The cavernous interior has the feel of a saloon out of *Lonesome Dove*, with screened doors, a wood-plank floor, and big fans over the entryway in lieu of air-conditioning. Down one wall, under the beer signs, a long bulletin board is feathered with business cards dating back decades, some of them so faded you can't read them anymore. Wayne Mueller, Louie's grandson, inherited the business and has continued the tradition of signaling that the restaurant is open for business by raising a U.S. flag outside. When he runs out of barbecue, not an uncommon occurrence, he hangs a sign on the door that says "Out of Meat" and lowers the colors. I visited Mueller's twice before I actually got to eat there, it's so popular.

Thirty miles away in Lexington, at Snow's BBQ, they have turned the laws of supply-and-demand into a full-blown mystique. Snow's is open only on Saturday—"8 a.m. to sold out!"—and started drawing crowds after *Texas Monthly* named it the best barbecue joint in the state in 2008. Part of the attraction is meeting the pitmaster, a snowy-haired woman named Tootsie Tomanetz, still shoveling hot coals well into her eighties.

From Lexington in the east to Llano in the west, central Texas is studded with exemplary barbecue. The place that has the greatest reputation for it is in the heart of the heart: Lockhart, a picturesque Victorian town of thirteen thousand that counts four major barbecue restaurants. One of them, Black's, claims to be the oldest barbecue restaurant in Texas run by the same family. Two of the others, Kreuz and Smitty's, are owned by branches of the same clan and figured in one of the most publicized disputes in Texas barbecue history.

Edgar "Smitty" Schmidt, a longtime butcher for Kreuz, bought the place with the unique open-floor barbecue pit in 1948 and ran it for thirty-six years. It was an old-fashioned meat market where you ordered beef by the pound, and it came on brown butcher paper with no sides except pickles, onions, and saltines or white bread. No barbecue sauce. For years, there weren't any utensils either; you sliced your beef with a knife chained to the middle of one of the communal tables. Only when customers started taking the knives as souvenirs did the market offer plastic cutlery.

In 1984 Schmidt sold Kreuz to his sons, Don and Rick. When he died in 1990, he left the building that housed the market to his daughter, Nina Sells. Eight years later, Nina and her brother Rick, who owned the business by then, had a falling-out over a rental extension and property repairs. "Most of the stories that came out about it, they called it a feud," Rick remembered, "and it wasn't a feud."

Whatever it was, it was enough to make Kreuz vacate its home of almost a hundred years. Rick Schmidt built a new restaurant four blocks away, one of the largest barbecue places in Texas, seating six

Hot links on the pit in Lockhart, Texas, 2011.

The "no sauce" sign at Kreuz Market, Lockhart, Texas. Kreuz relented and started offering sauce in 2018.

Signage for Black's, in the barbecue mecca of Lockhart, Texas.

hundred, and filled it with artifacts from the old haunt and reminders of its quaint ways like the sign that says "No Barbecue Sauce (Nothing To Hide)." Three weeks after the new Kreuz debuted in 1999, his sister Nina reopened the former market as Smitty's, named for their father, and carried on with her son as the new pitmaster. Both restaurants have done well.

In fact, the Lockhart name has become quite a calling card in the barbecue world. A Schmidt relative in Dallas started a well-regarded restaurant there, Lockhart Smokehouse. Younger kin collaborated on a place in Bee Cave, outside Austin, called Schmidt Family Barbecue. And a Lockhart native living in New York opened Hill Country Market BBQ, a hit restaurant there, which bolstered its cred by selling Kreuz sausage.

In the end, a little controversy was good for business. But good barbecue was even better.

Texas barbecue in recent years has gone from an obsession to something approaching a cult. People stand in line for hours at the hottest new places and worry that the barbecue will run out before they get in the door. Spaces at Camp Brisket and Barbecue Summer Camp, continuing education seminars offered by Texas A&M and the Foodways Texas organization, sell out within minutes. *Texas Monthly* launched an annual barbecue festival in Austin and made national news in

In this 1954 magazine ad, tied in with the *Annie Oakley* TV show, Canada Dry touted a cowgirl barbecue that featured hamburgers and hot dogs but no brisket.

COL. ZACK'S BARBECUE SAUCE

ORIGINATED & MANUFACTURED ON THE
101 RANCH
PONCA CITY, OKLAHOMA.

Made from CHOICE
VEGETABLES, FRUITS,
IMPORTED & DOMESTIC
SPICES, WALNUTS and
INDIAN SAGE

SOLD BY LEADING
GROCERS AND
STORES, the BEST
HOTELS and CAFES

Zack Miller of the 101 Ranch in Oklahoma staged a touring Wild West show like Buffalo Bill's from 1905 to 1931 and sold his own brand of barbecue sauce.

THE OTHER RANCH BARBECUE

There's another kind of cowboy barbecue out west, although nobody calls it that.

Santa Maria–style barbecue dates to the first half of the 1800s when California was part of Mexico and ranches would celebrate the completion of a cattle drive with feasts of beef roasted over fiery trenches.

The custom lived on in the Santa Maria Valley, on the Central Coast, where it became a localized type of grilling. In the modern version, chunks of beef are rubbed with salt, pepper, and garlic salt, skewered, and then grilled over red oak coals. The preferred cut is tri-tip, the bottom part of the sirloin. It's served with small pink beans that grow in the area called pinquitos.

Santa Maria barbecue has had a couple of moments in the national spotlight. The Los Compadres cooking team catered Santa Maria barbecues for President Ronald Reagan five times when he was in the White House. And much of the action in the 2004 movie *Sideways* was set at the Hitching Post II in the town of Buellton, one of several restaurants in the area that specialize in the dish.

Still, Santa Maria is hardly as famous as Texas brisket or Carolina pork. *Sunset* magazine food editor Margo True called it "America's least-known best barbecue."

Will Rogers barbecuing at his ranch in Santa Monica, California, 1920s.

Santa Maria Barbecue

California's native barbecue uses beef tri-tip, a triangular-shaped cut from the bottom of the sirloin. As the dish has received more national attention, it has become easier to find tri-tip in stores—but you still might need to order it from a butcher. This recipe comes from the Santa Maria Valley Chamber of Commerce, which wants the whole world to know about its barbecue specialty.

Serves 8

2 cups oak chips
2 tablespoons granulated garlic
1 tablespoon kosher salt
1 teaspoon black pepper
1 beef tri-tip, at least 2 pounds, with fat on one side

Soak oak chips in water for at least an hour. In a small bowl, mix the dry ingredients and rub onto the meat on all sides. Let stand at least half an hour at room temperature. Prepare a medium-size fire on one side of a grill. Just before cooking, add chips to induce smoke. Set the meat over the fire, fat side up, and brown well, about 10 minutes on each side. Move the tri-tip away from the coals, cover the grill, and cook indirectly for at least half an hour, until the meat registers 140°F internally on a thermometer. Transfer the tri-tip to a cutting board and let rest for a few minutes. Slice across the grain.

2013 when it hired the first full-time barbecue editor at a major publication, Daniel Vaughn, an architect turned food writer.

The magazine has long championed Texas barbecue, and the special issue it devotes to the subject, listing the state's fifty best barbecue places, is as anticipated and debated as the college football season. The only thing everyone agrees on is the proposition that barbecue is better in Texas. Here's how the magazine introduced its 2013 roster:

> The 50 BEST BBQ JOINTS . . . in the World!
> Our definitive, soot-stained guide to the best purveyors of smoked meat in Texas—which is to say, the best purveyors of smoked meat on Earth.

Nobody brags about barbecue like a Texan.

Of course, they've had a lot to brag about. A new generation of back-to-the-roots barbecue places have sprung up in Texas, mostly in the big cities, reflecting a broader interest in the intricacies of smoke-cooking: restaurants like La Barbecue in Austin, Corkscrew in Houston, and Smoke and Pecan Lodge in Dallas.

A corrugated metal barbecue stand in Corpus Christi, Texas, 1939.

The avatar of craft barbecue is Aaron Franklin, a former rock drummer in Austin who began peddling out of a food trailer in 2009. Word about his amazing brisket quickly circulated—*Texas Monthly* called him a "barbecue savant"—and the restaurant that followed, Franklin Barbecue, has sold out of meat consistently from the time it opened.

With his black glasses and his intermittent dark stubble, looking every inch the barbecue nerd, Franklin became famous for his attention to detail, for tinkering with the fire and experimenting with placement of the brisket. "We pitmasters are more thermal engineers than we are cooks," he wrote in his 2015 book, *Franklin Barbecue: A Meat-Smoking Manifesto*, which one reviewer called a two-hundred-page recipe for brisket. He demonstrated his techniques in a public TV series.

The line to get into Franklin Barbecue grew so long that it became a story itself. The *New York Times* wrote about the scene outside the restaurant, where people would gather early in the morning and wait as much as four or five hours. "This is the white whale of barbecue," explained one man, who was making his third attempt at Moby Dick before flying home to Los Angeles. The restaurant had run out of meat the other times.

Franklin Barbecue Brisket

Can you smoke a brisket at home that's as good as the brisket people stand in long lines for at Franklin Barbecue in Austin, Texas? Maybe, if you sweat the details like pitmaster Aaron Franklin. This recipe is adapted from his instructional videos and his 2015 book *Franklin Barbecue: A Meat-Smoking Manifesto*.

1 brisket, about 12 pounds
¼ cup kosher salt
¼ cup ground black pepper
    (16-mesh grind)
Granulated garlic,
    granulated onion, paprika
    (all optional)
Spray bottle of water,
    vinegar, or other liquid

Trim refrigerated brisket (it's easier to cut when it's cold) until the fat cap is ¼ to ½ inch thick. Apply salt-and-pepper rub (you can add those other seasonings if you like, but you don't have to) evenly on all surfaces. Be careful that none of it builds up in crevices or dimples. Let brisket warm up to room temperature, about an hour.

Start your fire. Franklin devotes a hundred pages in his book to fires and smokers, but we're going to keep it simple here. He prefers an offset cooker with oak burned down to embers. When the smoker reads around 275°F, place the brisket on the grate with the fat side up and the point facing the fire. Place a bowl of water between the fire and the brisket to help moisturize the meat.

Keep the lid closed for the first 3 hours. After that, start checking the brisket every 20 to 30 minutes, spritzing it with liquid from the spray bottle. Around 6 hours, the fat cap should be rendering and the outer layer should be developing a dark bark. When this happens, remove the brisket and wrap it in butcher paper. Return it to the cooker.

At about 10 hours, feel the brisket. If it's done, it should be soft and pliable. Check the internal temperature with a meat thermometer, and if it's between 190° and 200°F, remove the brisket. Let it rest wrapped for an hour, then slice against the grain and serve.

President Barack Obama visited Austin's Franklin Barbecue in 2014, drawing a mild rebuke for cutting in the long line.

Sonny Bryan, founder of a Dallas barbecue dynasty.

One visitor who checked Franklin off his barbecue bucket list was President Barack Obama, who stirred considerable comment when he dropped into the restaurant in 2014 and apologetically cut ahead of everyone else. A typical reaction on Twitter: "Apparently Obama skipped the line at Franklin's BBQ today. DICK move, bro!" When Kanye West tried the same tactic later, management told him no.

Aaron Franklin received the food world's official benediction in 2015 when the James Beard Foundation named him the best chef in the Southwest. The best chef! It was the first time a pitmaster had won the recognition, taking an award that usually went to people who cooked at establishments that didn't post their menu on a blackboard or have beer advertising all over the walls. (A second pitmaster, Rodney Scott of South Carolina, won an equivalent Beard award in 2018—more on that later.)

The foundation had actually honored six barbecue places before with its America's Classics award, which goes to less expensive eating places that have stood the test of time, like diners, pizza parlors, and pancake houses. There were two recipients in Texas (Louie Mueller in Taylor and the Original Sonny Bryan's in Dallas), two in North Carolina (the Skylight Inn in Ayden and Lexington Barbecue No. 1

5673-51 E

in Lexington), one in Arkansas (Jones Bar-B-Q Diner in Marianna), and one in Virginia (Doumar's Barbecue in Norfolk, which is better known for its part in creating the ice cream cone).

But those prizes were different. Daniel Vaughn compared them to winning a Lifetime Achievement award at the Oscars; Franklin's was like winning Best Actor.

"This award is so much bigger than me and so much bigger than our restaurant in Austin, Texas," the tuxedoed honoree said at the banquet. "It's pretty huge for barbecue in general."

In Texas, they were not the least bit surprised that one of theirs was first.

Barbecue under the desert sky of Arizona, 1951.

5
Pig Sandwiches

In a nation of neon pigs, the dapper porker on the sign above Leonard's Barbecue in Memphis might be the most illustrious of them all.

The restaurant was founded in 1922 as a five-stool lunch counter and grew to become one of the largest drive-ins in the country. The neon sign out front stands as an archetypal example of what might be called the "Why Is This Pig Smiling?" genre of outdoor advertising. It shows a cartoon swine wearing a tailcoat, twirling a cane, a top hat jauntily cocked behind one pointed ear. At night, his legs move and he appears to be strolling down the avenue like a swell from a Fred Astaire movie. "Mr. Brown goes to town," reads the slogan, using the founder's slang for charred outside meat. Judging from his happy expression, Mr. Brown seems unaware that *he* might be on the menu.

Leonard's went to considerable expense to have the sign moved and restored when the business relocated to the southern edge of Memphis. "I keep it running all night because I like to drive up in the morning and see him there waiting," the owner, Dan Brown (no relation), told me when I visited before the lunch rush. "I hate to think what it's costing me."

Brown started at Leonard's as a teenager, in 1962, slicing onions and then graduating to become a sandwich man. That meant he was entrusted with the foundation of Memphis barbecue: a hamburger bun heaped with chopped pork shoulder, anointed with barbecue sauce, and topped with coleslaw. Many people in Memphis don't even call it a sandwich; they call it "a barbecue."

Brown was working at the restaurant when its most famous customer would drop by for a late-night barbecue. Elvis Presley tried

OPPOSITE: At Leonard's in Memphis, once the largest barbecue restaurant in America, an elegant neon pig has twirled his walking cane for decades.

visiting during regular hours, but his celebrity made that impractical and he arranged to have Leonard's stay open for him after closing time. The King and his court would arrive around midnight and repair to a semiprivate room called the Pig Pen while Brown and others kept the kitchen running to serve them. Fans soon caught on.

"Word got around that if you saw cars at Leonard's half an hour after we had closed, Elvis might be coming in," Brown said. "They'd be waiting for him. He'd get mobbed just trying to get in the door."

After a while, Elvis gave up and had one of his entourage come for takeout. He wasn't going to miss out on his barbecue.

Memphis didn't create the barbecue restaurant any more than Elvis created rock 'n' roll. But just as the man with the swivel hips came to embody the music, the city on the bluff above the Mississippi epitomized the way barbecue moved in from the country and transitioned into a commercial enterprise. The process was well under way before Leonard's came along.

One of the forerunners of the barbecue restaurant was the private barbecue club, typically a group of gentlemen who would get together several times a year to feast on meat at a clubhouse or on a barbecue ground—sort of the pop-up dinners of their time. There were barbecue clubs in South Carolina as early as the late 1700s. Sumter County, Alabama, has a long history of them that continues to this day. The *Atlanta Constitution* mentioned two in the late 1800s. One, the Cold Springs 'Cue Club in East Point, was run by a gifted pitmaster and Brunswick stew maker named John Thomas Ware, whose services were sought in distant cities. The other, known simply as the Q Club, was the subject of an 1891 feature whose headline claimed that it was "Something Entirely New and Original in the Festive Line" and "The Only Barbecue Club on Earth." Wrong on both counts. (That newspaper was my employer for many years; consider this a very belated correction.)

Barbecue men certainly sold smoked meat during the nineteenth century; they just didn't do it in regular dining establishments. In North Carolina (as we saw in chapter 2), the ancestors of the Skylight Inn family in Ayden cooked pigs for profit at church assemblies in the 1800s. In Texas (chapter 4), butchers at the Southside Market in Elgin peddled smoked sausage as early as the 1880s. In Kentucky, an Owensboro man named Harry Green ran a barbecue business from

his house starting in 1890. Other barbecuists, as the papers sometimes called them, marketed their food at fairs and public celebrations and catered events.

It's impossible to know exactly when and where the first barbecue restaurant opened, but from available evidence, reasonable facsimiles were operating out of informal street stands during the 1890s. Culinary historian Robert Moss believes the earliest ones may have opened in Texas and North Carolina. He cites two 1897 newspaper stories from Dallas about grease fires breaking out in barbecue stands there, and an 1899 notice in Charlotte about a woman renting a store where her husband planned to cook and sell barbecue.

There's another claim that predates those by a few years. Golden Rule, a chain of barbecue restaurants in the Birmingham, Alabama, area, traces its history to a rest stop in Irondale, on the road to Atlanta, where travelers stopped for pork plates and refreshments going back to 1891. Asked about the name more than a century later, Michael Matsos, the longtime owner, speculated that the original proprietors "must have been reading the Bible or something."

Meanwhile, in downtown Atlanta, a proper sit-down restaurant known for barbecue opened in 1900. Verner's was a full-service cafe

Many early barbecue places started as gas stations. Frenchie's, in Melrose, Louisiana, sold gas, groceries, booze, *and* barbecue when Marion Post Wolcott photographed it in 1940.

with other dishes, but Andrew Marshall Verner was known primarily for smoked meats and Brunswick stew. Newspaper stories refer to his "well-known barbecue restaurant on Broad Street" and to him as "the barbecue connoisseur" and "the 'cue expert." His obituary, in 1934, said that Verner had traveled widely overseeing public barbecues and had cooked for as many as ten thousand people at one event.

By the time Verner died, hundreds of barbecue restaurants had opened in the South and Southwest and in bordering states like Missouri. Many of them started as sidelines to other businesses selling groceries or catering to the growing number of traveling motorists at filling stations and tourist courts. Sprayberry's in Newnan, Georgia, was a service station until the barbecue outsold the gasoline and took over the place in 1926. McClard's in Hot Springs, Arkansas, was a tourist court and gas station before barbecue became its focus in 1928.

Fresh Air, on U.S. 23 in Jackson, Georgia, was typical of the roadside barbecue joints that sprung up during the 1920s and '30s. Toots Caston ran the place for years.

Another roadside pioneer: Bozo's Hot Pit Bar-B-Q opened in 1923 on U.S. 79 in Mason, Tennessee.

Some of the most iconic barbecue joints in America appeared during the early road food boom of the 1920s and '30s: the Dixie Pig in Blytheville, Arkansas (1923); Bozo's in Mason, Tennessee (1923); Abe's in Clarksdale, Mississippi (1924); Big Bob Gibson's in Decatur, Alabama (1925); Fresh Air in Jackson, Georgia (1929); Stamey's in Greensboro, North Carolina (1930); Van's Pig Stand in Shawnee, Oklahoma (1930).

Van's wasn't the only Pig Stand. A chain by that name—the Pig Stands—started in Texas almost a decade earlier. The first location opened on the highway between Dallas and Fort Worth in September 1921, the same month White Castle began selling hamburgers in Kansas. Both businesses pioneered the coming wave of fast food in America, but the Pig Stands were notable for something else: they were among the first drive-ins.

Jessie G. Kirby, a tobacco and candy wholesaler in Dallas, conceived the restaurant when he noticed that "people with cars are so lazy they don't want to get out of them to eat." He and his financial partner, physician Reuben Jackson, designed a simple barbecue stand where customers could pull over to the side of the road and tell waiters what they wanted at the curb—literally curb service. Soon they added parking lots where the servers became known as carhops for the way they jumped on the running boards of moving automobiles to take orders.

The Pig Stands barbecue chain started in Texas and grew to more than a hundred locations by the early 1930s. The advertising slogan was direct: "Eat a Pig Sandwich."

By the early 1930s, there were more than a hundred Pig Stands in a southern swath running from Florida to California. The sign of the silhouetted pig became a familiar sight to the second generation of American motorists. Perhaps it was ironic that a chain born in Texas, the home of barbecued beef, would be named for pork. But it was. The Pig Stand slogan—"Eat a Pig Sandwich"—referred to its main menu item: a hamburger bun filled with barbecued pork and a slaw-like relish.

It was, essentially, a Memphis barbecue sandwich.

Memphis was ideally situated to sire barbecue joints. As the capital of the Delta, the vast river bottomlands of western Tennessee, eastern Arkansas, and northwestern Mississippi, the city attracted legions of African American farm folk who had intimate experience with smoking pigs. The city drew the same sorts of people who seeded the barbecue cultures that would flourish in Kansas City, St. Louis, and Chicago. For many of them, Memphis was an initial stop.

"In Memphis, particularly in the black sections of the city, barbecue pits are more common than lawn furniture," Lolis Eric Elie commented many years later in his barbecue travelogue *Smokestack Lightning.*

Many of the early barbecue places in Memphis were run by African Americans: spots like Culpepper's, Jim's Rib Shack, and Johnny Mills off Beale Street, the main drag of black life in the city. Johnny Mills was especially celebrated. The restaurant invited white patrons with separate dining areas for both races, and stars like Frank Sinatra and Bing Crosby would stop by when they were in town performing. Sam Phillips, the music producer who would later discover Elvis Presley, used to smell the barbecue smoke from the roof of the Peabody Hotel, where he produced big band radio broadcasts during the 1940s. "You couldn't get too mad or too drunk not to smell Johnny Mills barbecue, even when the wind was blowing in the other direction," he remembered. "Oh, God, I went to Johnny Mills as often as I could."

But most white people in the age of segregation didn't hang out on Beale Street. For them, the most popular barbecue places in town were the drive-ins: Berretta's, the Pig 'n Whistle (one of two chains with that name in the South), and the biggest one of all, Leonard's.

Leonard Heuberger was the son of German immigrants who ran a saloon in downtown Memphis. When he returned from World War I, he got into the business himself and opened a lunch counter that served barbecue and beer (or "Bar-beer-que" as the front window beckoned in one photo from the era). In 1932, he moved to a larger location on Bellevue Boulevard, whose southern extension would be known years later as Elvis Presley Boulevard, and turned it into a drive-in.

At its peak, during the 1950s, Leonard's could seat three hundred customers and employed as many as twenty carhops to serve more than a hundred automobiles under long metal sheds surrounding the restaurant. The barbecue was cooked over charcoal and hickory in a stand-alone brick building out back, overseen by a handful of African American pitmasters like Paul Tappin and James Willis. "We sell more barbecue than any restaurant in the world," the menu boasted.

Heuberger was deft at customer relations and marketing. He was the one who conceived the strutting pig marquee, which was built by the Balton Sign Company, which also did the iconic Holiday Inn spectacular of the 1950s. Heuberger called his pig Mr. Brown because he had noticed that men seemed to like the dark outside meat more, while women preferred the lighter inside meat. He had matchbooks, playing cards, and other promotional materials made showing two cartoon porkers—Mr. Brown Pig and Miss White Pig—flirtatiously smiling at each other over a dinner table.

But it was his wife, Edith Heuberger, who is said to have come up with one of the inspirations that defines Memphis barbecue. One day

The staff at Leonard's Barbecue
in Memphis, 1930s.

early on, the story goes, the restaurant was running low on meat when she had the idea of stretching it by putting coleslaw on the sandwich. They've come that way ever since. In the rest of the country, except in parts of the Carolinas, you have to ask for slaw to be put on a barbecue sandwich; in Memphis, you have to ask for it *not* to be.

Dan Brown started at Leonard's near the end of its glory days. He had a Memphis native's deep attachment to barbecue. The only time his mother ever spanked him, he recalled, was when he disobeyed her instructions never to cross a busy four-lane near their home, because he wanted to go to the barbecue place on the other side after school. When she asked him where he had been and he denied his transgression, she noticed the sauce on his shirt. Punishment followed swiftly.

Brown worked at Leonard's for three years in the early 1960s, never imagining that it might become his career. He didn't particularly enjoy summertimes in the kitchen, which was not air-conditioned, and he found it worrisome that some of the other sandwich men were missing fingertips after all those years of wielding sharp knives.

He left for college in 1965 and was drafted into the army after that. When he returned five years later, he took a part-time job at Leonard's while he was finishing his education. This time, he had a new boss.

Leonard Heuberger had toyed with the idea of franchising, but he decided to sell the restaurant instead in 1968 and retire. The new owners were an investment group headed by a Chevy dealer that had plans to replicate Leonard's far and wide.

Souvenirs of the early 1970s, when Leonard's wanted to become a national chain.

Franchising seemed to be in the air. Tops, a Memphis chain that began in 1952, showed that a modest number of barbecue restaurants in a limited area could work logistically. Two other franchise operations, Loeb's and Coleman's, had plans for dozens of outlets. The new team at Leonard's were even more ambitious. They wanted to go national and adopted a slogan that showed what they had in mind: "As Memphis Knows, So Will America."

"They wanted to make this into the McDonald's of barbecue," Brown said. "It took them a long time to realize that barbecue wasn't fast food."

BARBECUE CHAINS

The world's largest restaurant chain began as a barbecue drive-in.

In 1940, Richard and Maurice McDonald opened McDonald's Barbecue in San Bernardino, California. Eight years later, frustrated by the hassles of providing service and the low profit margins of barbecue, they retooled the place as a walk-up hamburger stand—and you know the rest.

Barbecue has a long and fitful history with franchising. Although the Pig Stands chain was one of the early successes during the 1920s, it faded after World War II and retreated to a few locations in Texas. While the last one closed in 2006, one former outlet, in San Antonio, stayed open as a diner when a longtime waitress bought it and rechristened it Mary Ann's Pig Stand.

Barbecue does not lend itself to franchise standardization as easily as short-order fare like burgers. It seems the antithesis of fast food, with its emphasis on slow cooking and craft. For a long time, the only barbecue chain with more than a hundred locations was Sonny's, which started in Florida in 1968 and spread out along the interstate highways.

A growing number of franchise operations have started to crack the code in recent years. The biggest by far, Texas-based Dickey's, has some six hundred stores. Other successful chains include Famous Dave's of Minnesota, Mission BBQ of Maryland, and Shane's Rib Shacks of Georgia.

An early menu at McDonald's in San Bernardino, California, a barbecue drive-in before it retooled as a hamburger joint in 1948.

When Brown returned to Leonard's in 1970, the curb-service traffic had dwindled and the restaurant was becoming more of a sit-down place. The new ownership eventually opened ten other locations around Memphis—Brown went into management and ran many of them—but the majority had closed by the mid-1980s. The Loeb's and Coleman's chains were faltering too. A new Memphis restaurant with franchise aspirations, Corky's, was just starting up, but its growth would be more measured.

Leonard's finally shuttered the old drive-in in 1991. By then its flagship restaurant was in a newer building a few miles south, in a suburban area that felt safer to longtime customers. Brown bought

Shane's raised eyebrows when it began in the Atlanta suburbs in 2002. Its founder, Shane Thompson, said he wanted to create an environment for soccer moms who didn't like the funkiness of old-line barbecue joints. The meat was cooked on electric smokers for a lighter smoke flavor, and the decor was noticeably absent of porcine bric-a-brac. An early slogan promised "no pigs, no pits." While some might find that sacrilegious, there was evidently a market for Barbecue Lite; Shane's grew to more than seventy restaurants in ten states.

Other barbecue chains have embraced pigs and smoke. Alabama-based Jim 'n Nick's, with more than thirty restaurants in the Southeast and Colorado, has drawn good reviews for its barbecue. City Barbeque, out of Dublin, Ohio, boasts that the cookers at its four dozen locations never stop smoking. Moe's Original Bar B Que, based in Vail, Colorado, uses gas-assisted Ole Hickory smokers to good effect at its more than sixty outlets.

Even so, most purists are inherently suspicious of chain barbecue because it doesn't fit their ideal of authenticity. "I could have sold a hundred franchises if I'd wanted to," said Mike Mills, three-time grand champion of the Memphis in May contest and the operator of a renowned barbecue restaurant in Murphysboro, Illinois, the 17th Street Bar & Grill. "I didn't want to do that because I wanted to stay true to my product. Some chains put out a decent product, but it's not top of the line."

Dickey's started as a single restaurant in Dallas in 1941 and grew to become the nation's largest barbecue chain, with more than five hundred outlets.

the business in 1993 and redecorated the interior with reminders of its long and colorful history: old photos, a mural showing Leonard behind the counter, a 1950s delivery van parked in the middle of the dining room. But the best souvenir was out front where the famous pig sign—"Mr. Brown goes to town"—twirled his neon cane.

There was another memorable neon sign at Leonard's, one that showed a pig lying on its side over a bed of coals, looking strangely contented as if it were lounging in a sauna. Brown intended to have that sign restored and remounted as well, but shortly after Leonard's moved, vegan activists targeted the restaurant. They superglued the

The Busy Bee, a
storefront barbecue
place in Chattanooga,
Tennessee, 1920s.

Sox's Bar-B-Q, an
early food truck in
Columbia, South
Carolina, circa 1950.

Jack Walton's Hot Barbecue, part of a small chain in Texas, 1950.

The Bagley family, cooks and servers at Turnage's Barbecue in Durham, North Carolina, 1960s.

locks, sent threatening letters, and scraped "Meat Is Murder" on the outside of the building.

Given the circumstances, Brown decided that a neon pig roasting in flames might not be a prudent image just then. "We kept that one in storage."

While Leonard's is the granddaddy of Memphis barbecue restaurants, it's only a small part of a barbecue scene that is probably unmatched by any other municipality not named Kansas City. The Memphis area has barely 60 percent of the population of its rival, but it has almost as many barbecue restaurants. Some of them have national reputations.

Jim Neely's Interstate Bar-B-Que started in the 1970s and spawned several other restaurants run by family members. Raymond Robinson's Cozy Corner won acclaim for its barbecued Cornish game hen; after he died, his widow, Desiree Robinson, ran the pits with their children and grandchildren. Payne's Bar-B-Q, known for its chopped pork sandwich, was another widowed restaurant. Horton Payne, who opened the place with his mother in 1972, died a dozen years later, leaving his wife, Flora Payne, and their children to step in.

And then there's the most renowned barbecue place in town, the Rendezvous, the restaurant that started all the talk about dry-ribs-versus-wet that many people associate with Memphis. Charlie Vergos opened the Rendezvous in 1948 as a basement tavern in downtown Memphis, but it didn't hit its stride until he discovered a hidden coal

The Payne family of Payne's Bar-B-Que in Memphis. Flora Payne runs the restaurant with her children, Candice and Ron.

Charlie Vergos at the Rendezvous in Memphis, one of the most famous barbecue places in America and creator of "dry" ribs.

Memphis Dry Rib Rub

The Vergos family at the Rendezvous in downtown Memphis invented "dry ribs," using a blend of seasonings instead of the customary red finishing sauce. Now you can find dry ribs all over Memphis— and America. Here's a typical rub used in their preparation.

Makes about 2 cups

½ cup paprika
¼ cup chili powder
¼ cup granulated garlic
3 tablespoons ground black pepper
3 tablespoons kosher salt
1 tablespoon whole yellow mustard seed
1 tablespoon whole celery seeds
1 tablespoon crushed celery seeds
1 tablespoon dried oregano
1 tablespoon dried thyme
1 tablespoon whole allspice berries
1 tablespoon ground allspice
1 tablespoon whole coriander seed
1 tablespoon ground coriander

Combine seasonings and sprinkle over ribs before putting them on the smoker or grill and again at the end of cooking.

chute in the wall and converted it into a barbecue pit. He cooked his pork ribs with a dry rub sprinkled on after they were grilled. The "dry ribs"—not his term— confused some diners. "When I see a customer pick up a sauce bottle," said veteran waiter Jack Dyson, "I say try the Rendezvous style before you go to the sauce. And most of the time, they'll say, 'Oh, that's better.'"

Tourists flocked to the Rendezvous, in part because it was located down an alley across from the city's grand old hotel, the Peabody. Presidents and celebrities like the Rolling Stones and Memphis native Justin Timberlake visited, and the once-smoky rathskeller expanded to three levels to accommodate the crowds. When people told him that the Rendezvous had the best barbecue in town, John Vergos, the son of the founder, would gently correct them. "Let me tell you something," he'd say. "There's good barbecue all over Memphis."

Some of it isn't even barbecue, strictly speaking. In addition to dry ribs and barbecue sandwiches with slaw, Memphis became known for spin-off novelties like barbecue spaghetti, barbecue nachos, and barbecue pizza. Coletta's, an Italian restaurant, created the latter during the 1950s because they were afraid people wouldn't eat something as unfamiliar as pizza unless they topped it with something familiar like barbecued pork.

Naturally, Elvis loved it.

As Americans hit the highway, some barbecue places promoted themselves like motels and tourist attractions with postcards. Among them: Oklahoma Joe's in Albuquerque, New Mexico; Big Bob Gibson in Decatur, Alabama; C. F. Weiss Drug Store and Barbecue in Brighton, Michigan; Juicy Q Drive-in in Mineola, Texas; Brand's Barbecue in Roseburg, Oregon; Baugh's Bar-B-Q in Evansville, Indiana.

OKLAHOMA JOE'S   On U. S. 66,   Where Tourists Meet

Ladies and Men's Rest Rooms   Albuquerque, N. Mex.

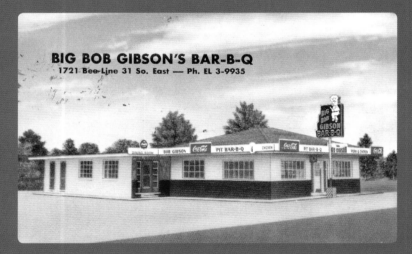

BIG BOB GIBSON'S BAR-B-Q
1721 Bee Line 31 So. East — Ph. EL 3-9935

BRAND'S—ON PACIFIC HIGHWAY 3 MILES NORTH OF ROSEBURG, ORE.   116410

"$20.00 Started VENTURE - NOW $$$100,000.00 Annual Sales!"

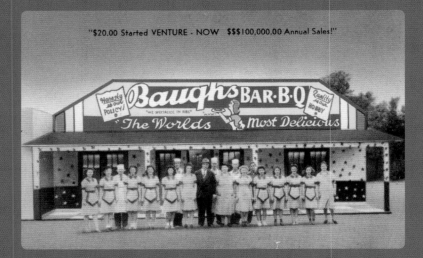

6

A Moveable Feast

Henry Perry didn't invent Kansas City barbecue, but you wouldn't know it from the way his adopted city claimed his life as a creation story many decades after he was gone.

Perry grew up with pit barbecue near Memphis and left Tennessee as a teenager to work as a steward and cook on the steamboats that plied the Mississippi and Missouri Rivers. In 1907 he settled in Kansas City and went to work in a saloon. The town was booming; it had become one of the nation's busiest rail hubs and its second largest meatpacking center. Growing numbers of southerners—black and white—were moving in. Perry saw an opportunity to give them a taste of home and started selling barbecue from a cart downtown. He did so well that he was soon able to open a restaurant in an old trolley barn.

There had been barbecues in the Kansas City area for years. Missouri had been a slave state, after all, and was familiar with plantation barbecues. Across the state line in Kansas, frontier barbecues like the ones in Texas were well known. In his autobiography, William F. Cody—Buffalo Bill—remembered attending an 1853 barbecue in Leavenworth that his father gave to befriend some Kickapoo Indians. In Kansas City itself, barbecues were usually big events celebrating Independence Day or some civic milestone like the opening of a bridge over the Missouri River.

Henry Perry represented something new. He is thought to have been the first man to run a commercial barbecue establishment in Kansas City, a place that became famous for them. Less than ten years after arriving, he was running ads in a local newspaper touting

Old barbecue sign in the 18th and Vine historic district in Kansas City, 2010.

himself as "Henry Perry, the Barbecue King . . . who is endowed with the gift to cook meat."

Perry went on to open two more restaurants and train many pitmasters who moved on to other barbecue places. Among them were two men who became instrumental in establishing the city's most enduring barbecue dynasties: Gates Bar-B-Q and Arthur Bryant's Barbeque.

"Kansas City might not even be Kansas City if not for Henry Perry," Doug Worgul wrote in *The Grand Barbecue*, his 2003 book about the city's pit heritage. "If somebody other than Henry Perry had been the first to open a barbecue joint in Kansas City, God might just have gotten exasperated and decided, 'Look, if you can't get it right, I'll let some other city be The Barbecue Capital of the World.'"

And make no mistake about it: Kansas City regards itself as the barbecue capital of the world.

Henry Perry stood at the leading edge of a demographic upheaval that would spread the gospel of barbecue across the nation.

At the beginning of the twentieth century, barbecue was still largely a regional phenomenon of the South and Southwest. That began to change when increasing numbers of southerners moved out of their homeland around the same time barbecue restaurants were coming into their own. In *The Southern Diaspora*, his history of that exodus, James N. Gregory estimated that almost 8 million black southerners, nearly 20 million white southerners, and 1 million southern-born Latinos left the region during the 1900s for other parts of the United States. They took their religion, their music, their distinctive accents—and of course their foods, one of the most characteristic of which was barbecue. At the peak of the shift, during World War II, *Life* magazine reported that Detroit and outlying towns were teeming with 200,000 white folks from the South who had come to work in the war industries and had brought "their barbecue stands and tent shouting evangelists." There were at least that many black folks there as well.

For many whites, the move away from the South was only temporary. For most African Americans, it was permanent. For that

reason—and because of their deep and abiding association with barbecue—they played a larger role in exporting it to the rest of the country.

The Great Migration of southern blacks started in the early 1900s, accelerated during World War I, slowed during the Depression, then took off during the 1940s and '50s. They were leaving the farms and small towns of the region for better job prospects, but they were just as eager to escape the racial injustice and violence of segregation.

The expatriates got into the barbecue business early on, opening street stands and takeout counters in scores of cities from New York to Los Angeles. Neighborhoods like Harlem and the South Side of Chicago soon smelled of barbecue smoke.

Not everyone approved of the newcomers and their down-home cooking. To some black people who had moved north and adjusted to the city, barbecue seemed like a countrified reminder of what they wanted to leave behind. "A great deal of complaint is heard in a so-called exclusive colored section of a rotisserie where barbecued pork and chicken, and, maybe, chitterlings are sold," a Chicago

The first panel of Jacob Lawrence's 1941 *Migration Series*, sixty paintings that depicted the mass move of African Americans from the South to the North. They took their barbecue culture with them. *The Phillips Collection, Washington, D.C.*

A barbecue block party in Harlem, 1978.

magazine with the curious name *Light and Heebie Jeebies* commented in 1927. "Some of the residents are up in arms, declaring that the place is a disgrace to such a district, and the words chitterling, barbecue, pig knuckle. and so forth are used with all their obnoxious connotative effect to produce a feeling of disgust in the mind of the person who reads about this rotisserie."

Around the same time, the *Messenger*, a magazine in Harlem, lamented that Kansas Citians would not support a fine black-owned hotel and restaurant but would rather eat pig meat. "Did colored Kansas City rush to fill it, to patronize this very creditable institution? No, it ran true to cultured, colored form. It went to the barbecue stands and the other places which had taken no such pains to supply comfort and catering to the race."

Anti-barbecue feelings more commonly took the form of religious strictures. After World War II, when the Muslim faith began

attracting adherents among African Americans, barbecued pork became a forbidden vestige of the life they were shedding. "Do not eat the swine—do not even touch it," warned Elijah Muhammad, the leader of the Nation of Islam, who had grown up with all manner of swine in Washington County, Georgia.

Despite such objections, barbecue flourished in the big cities of the North and the West for the simple reason that people who had been raised with it still loved it. Black entrepreneurs with southern roots catered to their hankering at restaurants like Wilson's in Pittsburgh, the Barbecue in New York, Park's Old Style in Detroit, Whitmore's in Cleveland, Daddy Bruce's in Denver, Everett & Jones in Oakland, Doc Hamilton's Barbeque Pit in Seattle, and many more.

No city exemplified the moveable feast like Chicago. From 1940 to 1960, its black population almost tripled as farm families from Mississippi, Arkansas, and Tennessee streamed into the South Side

The East Bay Dragons, a black bikers club, used to hang out at Helen's Bar-B-Que in Oakland, California, where this picture was shot in the early 1970s.

K.C. Classic Barbecue Sauce

Kansas City barbecue sauces weren't always sweet and thick, but the enormous success of the KC Masterpiece brand changed everyone's expectations. We used this recipe in 1995 in *The Ultimate Barbecue Sauce Cookbook*; it came from one of the pioneers of the cook-off circuit, Paul Kirk, who billed himself "the Kansas City Baron of Barbecue."

Makes about 4½ cups

¾ cup packed brown sugar
1 to 2 tablespoons ground black pepper
2 tablespoons chili powder
2 teaspoons dry mustard
1 teaspoon powdered ginger
½ teaspoon ground allspice
¼ teaspoon ground red pepper
¼ teaspoon ground mace
1 cup distilled white vinegar
¼ cup molasses
¼ cup water
1 (32-ounce) bottle ketchup
1 to 3 teaspoons liquid smoke (optional)

In a large saucepan, combine brown sugar, black pepper, chili seasoning, mustard, ginger, allspice, red pepper, and mace.

Add vinegar, molasses, and water. Stir until dry ingredients are dissolved. Stir in ketchup. Add liquid smoke if desired. Bring to a boil, stirring occasionally to avoid splattering. Reduce heat to low and simmer, covered, for 30 minutes. Stores for several weeks in an airtight jar in the refrigerator.

and retrofitted their rural barbecue ways for the city. It was the culinary equivalent of what was happening with their music, as the acoustic Delta blues got electrified and amped up with Mississippi-born artists like Muddy Waters and Howlin' Wolf. In acclimating themselves to their new home, the migrants created a new barbecue institution: the urban rib shack.

South Side rib shacks tended to be takeout places that catered to the night crowd. They had limited menus that ran toward hot link sausages and various cuts of ribs, especially rib tips, the short end pieces attached to cartilage instead of bone. They came on a pile of French fries, swimming in sweet barbecue sauce, with slices of white bread—a greasy, glorious mess.

Leon Finney, one of the pioneers of the genre, moved from Mississippi during the 1930s and got into the barbecue business almost accidentally when the restaurant where his aunt worked as a cook was busted for running a bookmaking operation. The owner offered to sell the place to her for $700. Her nephew found the money

BRAGGING RIGHTS

Kansas City claims to be the capital of the known barbecue universe, but there are a dozen other places that say the same thing. The contenders:

- In Tennessee, the state tourism bureau posted a page on its website titled "Barbecue Capital," lavishing attention on Memphis, where they consider themselves the kings of pork barbecue.
- In Texas, Lockhart—home of four classic pits—was recognized by the legislature as the state's barbecue capital. The town of Brady, with its World Championship Goat Cook-off, calls itself the goat barbecue capital.
- In Missouri, the Kansas City visitors bureau posted an article online declaring, "Kansas City Is the Barbecue Capital of the World." St. Louis cites its standing as the nation's top market for barbecue sauce.
- In Kentucky, Owensboro has the International Bar-B-Q Festival and the Moonlite Bar-B-Q Inn, where an oversized burgoo pot out front declares it "the Bar-B-Q Capital of the World."
- In California, the Santa Maria Valley markets itself as the center of ranch-style grilled beef.
- In Illinois, legislators named the town of Murphysboro as the barbecue capital because of a noted restaurant, the 17th Street Bar & Grill. The designation rankled people in Chicago, the spiritual home of the urban rib joint.
- In Georgia, *Life* magazine once named Newnan, the site of one of the state's venerable pits, Sprayberry's, as the barbecue capital.
- In South Carolina, the tourism bureau touted the state as "the birthplace of barbecue," and historian Lake E. High Jr. nominated Lexington County, home of several renowned barbecue places, as its epicenter.
- In North Carolina, the Skylight Inn in Ayden sports a capitol dome to dramatize its claim as the barbecue capital. Over in the Piedmont, Lexington holds a BBQ Capital Cook-off and a barbecue festival, and counts seventeen barbecue restaurants in a town of 18,993. That's one for every 1,117 residents, giving Lexington perhaps the highest 'cue rating in America.

The Moonlite Bar-B-Q Inn claims bragging rights for Owensboro, Kentucky.

Lem's Bar-B-Q in Chicago epitomized the spread of southern pit know-how. The Lemons brothers moved from Mississippi to Illinois and opened their first rib shack in the early 1950s, helping to create the city's barbecue culture.

One of the eccentricities of Chicago barbecue was the aquarium smoker, a glass-sided cooker where the ribs bathed in smoke like fish in water. This one was at Barbara Ann's BBQ on the South Side.

and opened Leon's Bar-B-Que in 1940. Among the most popular menu items were those chewy little rib tips. "Before we started buying them," Finney said, "meat wholesalers were throwing the back side of the rib cut away, as garbage."

Myles Lemons, who arrived from Indianola, Mississippi, in 1942, opened a rib shack called Lem's a decade later. It was one of the first in Chicago to use a new kind of cooking apparatus necessitated by the city's stricter regulations: an aquarium smoker, so named because the cooking area was enclosed in glass like a fish tank. The tempered walls funneled the smoke to a tall smokestack atop the building, lofting the exhaust farther away from the street. With a bank of takeout windows across the front and a smokestack on top, the Lem's on 75th Street looked like the captain's bridge on a steamboat.

For the most part, Lem's, Leon's, and others were cooking the same pork they had cooked in brick pits and trenches back in the South, but their new surroundings dictated a new approach to barbecue. "It was created from Mississippi," said James Lemons, Myles's younger brother, who ran Lem's for decades, "but it's Chicago barbecue."

In 1932, twenty-five years after he arrived in Missouri, Henry Perry was visited by a reporter for the *Kansas City Call*, one of the nation's oldest African American newspapers. The reporter found Perry in his flagship barbecue stand, at Nineteenth and Highland Streets, sitting in front of his pit tending the fire and turning the meat. Now fifty-seven, he was recovering from a stroke that had paralyzed one side of his body the year before, and he still walked with a limp. Even so, the visitor found him lively and talkative—especially about barbecue.

Perry said that a number of appliance makers had tried to interest him in using an easier modern cooking system. He wouldn't hear of it. "I told them that I wouldn't even have one of the things in my place. There is only one way to cook barbecue and that is the way I am doing it, over a wood fire, with a properly constructed oven and pit."

If there was any doubt the man was serious about his art, a sign on the wall dispelled it. "My business is to serve you," it said, "not to entertain you."

The reporter credited Perry with being the first person in America to turn barbecue into a profession, which wasn't quite true. "Until he introduced the style of cooking in a commercial way," the story read, "it was only used for special purposes—at the big camp meetings of

Chicago Rib Tips

Gnawing and sucking your way through a plate of pork rib tips is an essential part of the Chicago barbecue experience. Tips come from the lower end of spareribs and are usually trimmed off because they have so much cartilage. But those tubes of cartilage are separated by meat and fat, taking flavor to a new level by combining the meaty goodness of ribs with the fatty richness of pork belly. The best way to make rib tips—the way Chicago barbecue joints do them—is to cook an entire slab and then chop off the triangular tips. That helps keep them from drying out. This recipe comes from Craig "Meathead" Goldwyn, owner of the barbecue website AmazingRibs.com and author of the 2016 book *Meathead: The Science of Great Barbecue and Grilling*.

Makes 6 to 8 servings

THE RUB

¾ cup firmly packed dark brown sugar
¾ cup white sugar
½ cup paprika
¼ cup garlic powder
2 tablespoons ground black pepper
2 tablespoons ground ginger
2 tablespoons onion powder
2 teaspoons rosemary powder

THE MEAT

2 slabs pork rib tips, about 4 pounds
¼ teaspoon kosher salt per pound of meat
4 tablespoons apple juice
½ cup of your favorite BBQ sauce

Mix the rub ingredients thoroughly in a bowl. Season the tips with kosher salt. (Table salt is more concentrated than kosher salt, so if you use table salt, use half as much.) If you can, give the salt 1 to 2 hours to be absorbed. Then put on the rub. Use enough to cover the meat surface but still let some meat show through.

You can use a smoker or a grill. Prepare a smoker and get it up to about 225°F. On a charcoal grill, pour a chimney full of preheated charcoal briquets on one side of the grill's charcoal grate in order to create two heat zones, one hot zone with direct radiant heat, and an indirect heat convection zone. Adjust the vents to bring the temperature to about 225°F on the indirect side. On a gas grill, adjust the temperature knobs so that one half of the grill is off and the other half is heated enough to maintain a temperature of approximately 225°F on the indirect side. Add two or three chunks of your favorite smoking wood to the fire for flavor. If you have chips or pellets, use about half a cup.

Place the tips on the main cooking grate in the indirect heat zone as far away from the heat source as possible. On a charcoal grill, position the top vent directly above the tips in order to force the smoke over and around the meat. Allow the meat to cook for 2½ hours. No need to add more wood.

Now we come to the Texas Crutch, so called because some think it was invented there. No Chicago rib joint would bother with this step, but for home cooks, it helps make the meat more tender and juicy. If you decide to skip this step, just continue to cook the meat for another 45 minutes or so.

To do the Texas Crutch, lay out a double layer of heavy-duty aluminum foil, approximately 8 inches longer than the tips, for each of the slabs. Lay the tips, meat side down, in the center of the foil. Fold the sides of the foil up, being careful not to puncture it. Add 2 tablespoons of apple juice to each foil packet before tightly sealing. Place foiled ribs on the smoker or grill and cook for another 30 minutes.

Remove the foil packets from the cooker and cautiously open the foil to allow the steam to escape. Place the tips back on the smoker or grill. Cover and allow the tips to cook for approximately 15 minutes until the surface of the meat, called the "bark," has dried. Use the "bend test" to check for doneness: Pick up the slabs on one end with a pair of tongs and bounce them slightly. If they are ready, the bark and meat will crack a bit. Even if they don't crack, if you've kept the temperature around 225°, stop cooking after 4 hours.

Remove the tips from the smoker or grill. Using a cleaver or sharp chef's knife, hack them into 1-to-3-inch pieces. In Chicago, tips are usually doused with a sweet tomato barbecue sauce and served on top of a slice of white bread. But try them first; you may not want any sauce at all.

People in Kansas City really took to Dixiefied names when it came to barbecue, as this 1950s view of the Dixieland Bar-B-Q Drive-in shows.

the South, at political pow wows, and gatherings of that nature." It also credited Perry with starting a trend that had led to one thousand barbecue stands and restaurants in Kansas City, which *was* true, minus a zero. "The barbecue business," the reporter cracked, "is about as prolific in the Missouri city as saloons are in Tia Juana."

As for Perry's establishment, the *Call* described it as an egalitarian place that attracted blacks and whites and drew a mix of "swanky" limousines and inexpensive Model Ts. "Liveried chauffeurs gaze haughtily at humble self-drivers—but all have the common ambition to sink their teeth in a bit of Perry's succulent barbecue."

The Barbecue King lived another eight years, turning up in the local press only when he shot and critically wounded a prowler who had broken into the business looking for food. When he died in 1940, he left one of his restaurants to the man from Texas who had been managing it, Charlie Bryant. Charlie had a younger brother named Arthur.

The elevation of Kansas City barbecue to legendary status began in earnest with a single line in a 1972 magazine article. Calvin Trillin, a native who had gone on to become a noted writer in New York, wrote a food tour of his hometown for *Playboy* in which he poked fun at

SNOOTS IN THE 'LOU

There's another city in Missouri that developed a distinguished barbecue culture but seldom gets the attention Kansas City gets.

St. Louis has several claims to barbecue fame. For starters, it gave its name to a cut of pork: St. Louis ribs, a neat, squared-off version of spareribs with the tips trimmed off. Then there's the barbecue sauce connection: St. Louis birthed one of the first commercial sauces anywhere, Maull's. People apparently take its slogan seriously—"Don't baste your barbecue! You gotta Maull it!"—because market studies have shown that the city leads the nation in per capita consumption of barbecue sauce. That's probably because they like to douse it on the pork steaks that are a backyard grilling staple in Missouri.

St. Louis's most misunderstood barbecue specialty is snoots. The name conjures images of a disembodied pig snout, but the reality isn't quite that graphic. Snoots do come from the facial meat of the hog—which anyone who has had a hot dog has eaten—but it's sliced or chopped like any other barbecue.

I tried snoots for the first time at Big Mama's BBQ, across the river in East St. Louis, Illinois. The young woman behind the counter looked slightly amused as my wife and I examined the menu board and spoke softly about which snoot item we should order.

"Do you want to try a sample?" she asked.

"Sure," I said. "Do you get many people here who just want to try the snoots?"

"All the time."

She gave us a little plastic cup full of pork pieces like you'd find in a sliced barbecue sandwich, heavily sauced. They were on the crispy side and tasted earthy and salty, like pork rinds. As I ate them, I did not begin to snort.

"Did you like that?" she asked.

"Pretty well," I said—and ordered a chopped-pork sandwich.

the way civic boosters touted fancy expense-account restaurants and downplayed the humble cafes and chophouses that were closer to the city's bones. Places like his favorite barbecue spot. "It has long been acknowledged," Trillin wrote, "that the single best restaurant in the world is Arthur Bryant's Barbeque in Kansas City."

Pilgrims have been flocking to Bryant's—and all the other classic Kansas City barbecue places—ever since.

There are more than a hundred barbecue restaurants in the Kansas City area, serving a wider range of dishes than you'll find just about anywhere else—mostly beef and ribs, but increasingly pork. Some of them have been around for many decades, like Rosedale Bar-B-Q in Kansas City, Kansas, opened by Anthony Rieke and his wife and brother-in-law in 1934. Or Jack Stack Barbecue, started by the Fiorella family in 1957. Other choice places are newer, like LC's, opened in 1986 by Mississippi native L. C. Richardson, or Joe's Kansas City, spawned by a competition barbecue team in 1996.

Of all those operations, only two have bloodlines that go back to Kansas City's original barbecue royalty.

Gates Bar-B-Q, which grew to become a chain with half a dozen locations, started in 1946 when George Gates, a railroad waiter, bought a barbecue restaurant called Ol' Kentuck. The purchase came with the services of Arthur Pinkard, who had worked under Perry as a pitmaster. "Daddy knew how to cook barbecue for a family, but Mr. Arthur taught him the commercial side of it," remembered Ollie Gates, George's son.

Gates toiled in his father's kitchen as a teenager but did not enjoy it. "Barbecue was a dirty business. You'd get all this smoke in your eyes and smoke in your lungs. When I went off to college, I promised myself I'd never go into barbecue."

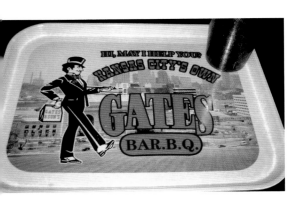

A 1970s serving tray from Gates Bar-B-Q. The Kansas City chain started in 1946 as Gates Ol' Kentuck Bar-B-Q.

But when he returned in 1956, something interesting was happening. Kansas City had always been known for steaks—all those stockyards and slaughterhouses—but it was starting to build a reputation for barbecue as well. The perception was shifting because of the publicity that came with major league baseball. The American League team in Philadelphia moved to town at the beginning of the 1955 season, and as luck would have it, the Kansas City Athletics played in a stadium near the Eighteenth and Vine District, where most of the jazz clubs and best barbecue places were located. Fans could smell the seductive fumes coming from Gates and other restaurants. "The announcers would talk about it, and they'd come in to eat along with the players," Gates said, "and I believe that's how Kansas City barbecue got introduced to the United States."

One of those nearby barbecue places that smelled so good was Arthur Bryant's. Arthur's brother, Charlie, who had worked with Henry Perry for years and took over one of his restaurants when the patriarch died, ran it for six years and then retired, handing if off to Arthur in 1946, the same year Gates opened. The two became pitched competitors, one known mainly in Kansas City, the other becoming, with the help of a certain writer, one of the most renowned barbecue joints in America.

And Bryant's *was* a joint. "He called it a grease house. People say when you used to come in here, you could just slide up to the counter,"

Arthur Bryant, 1975. He founded the Kansas City "grease house" that Calvin Trillin called the single best restaurant in the world.

said general manager Eddie Echols, who never worked for Bryant but grew up in the neighborhood and knew him well enough to know that he wasn't as grouchy as he looked.

Arthur Bryant's became famous for two things: a weirdly hot barbecue sauce and a magnificent beef brisket that left a by-product he called scraps but others called burnt ends. They were the crusty end pieces of the brisket, full of fat and char and spicy flavor, and he used to give them away. After Trillin wrote about them, people requested them and they eventually became a regular menu item around town. Now burnt ends are synonymous with Kansas City barbecue.

Bryant died in 1982 in the bed he kept in his office at the restaurant. He never married or had family. As one obituary writer put it, "Meat was [his] mistress." After he was gone, the restaurant modernized a bit, got some matching chairs, replaced the splintery tabletops, hung some photos of the many celebrity customers who made the trek to Brooklyn Avenue, including half a dozen presidents starting with Harry Truman.

"I don't think Mr. Bryant would appreciate some of the changes," Echols allowed. "He liked to keep dogs in here, and the health department wouldn't let us do that anymore. He'd miss his dogs."

In this 1954 postcard, a little snow didn't stop the people at the Northfield Inn in East Northfield, Massachusetts, from having a cookout.

But the brisket is still cooked over oak and hickory for at least ten hours, and the mess of fries it comes with are still dropped in vats of hot lard.

"He'd recognize the food. I think he'd still like the barbecue."

Near the end of that article extolling Arthur Bryant's, Calvin Trillin paid homage to Henry Perry in his usual droll manner. He said he'd like to ask the mayor and city council whether they had ever heard of Perry. They'd probably think he was talking about Commodore Perry, the American naval hero, so he'd set them straight and tell them about the father of Kansas City barbecue. Then he'd ask a pointed question:

"What I can't understand is why this town is full of statues of the farmers who came out to steal land from the Indians and full of statues of the businessmen who stole the land from the farmers but doesn't even have a three-dollar plaque somewhere for Henry Perry."

Forty-two years after that article, the American Royal Association, sponsors of a huge barbecue contest staged annually in Kansas City, began a Barbecue Hall of Fame and inducted Henry Perry.

It wasn't a statue, but it was a start.

CLOSE COVER BEFORE STRIKING

708 PINE ST.
ST. LOUIS, MO.

Taystee
BAR-B-Q

PHONE · GARFIELD · 9987

The Original

CHARCOAL BAR-B-Q
RIBS & CHICKEN

Universal Match Corp., St. Louis

BAR-B-Q

TAYSTEE

Phone: LI-0212

TAYSTEE
BAR-B-Q
OHIO AND
MASSACHUSETTS
INDIANAPOLIS

The Original Charcoal
Bar-B-Q Ribs & Chicken

Close Cover Before Striking Match

Close Cover Before Striking

234 W. FIRST ST., LOS ANGELES
in the Civic Center
Phone TUcker 2967

Restaurant — Cocktails

The REDWOOD HOUSE

BANQUET FACILITIES   Phone TUcker 2967

SMOKEY JOE'S

HICKORY
BARBECUE
RESTAURANTS

LOS ANGELES
NORTH HOLLYWOOD
SANTA MONICA

Universal Match Corp. Los Angeles

MATCH CORP. OF AMERICA · CHICAGO
MADE IN U.S.A.

KNOWN FROM COAST TO COAST

PORKY'S

Drop Your
(?WORRIES?)
Relax, Laugh
and have
FUN

at

★ CHOICE WINES & LIQUORS
★ SOUTHERN FRIED CHICKEN
★ RIBS

DINE and WINE at

PORKY'S
Finest
BAR-B-Q

1420 SO. ABERDEEN ST.
1100 WEST OFF 14th
CANAL 9362 · CHICAGO
THE TALK OF THE TOWN!

CLOSE COVER BEFORE STRIKING

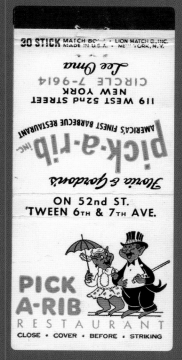

30 STICK MATCH BOOK · LION MATCH CO. INC.
MADE IN U.S.A. · NEW YORK, N.Y.

Lee Oma
CIRCLE 7-9614
NEW YORK
119 WEST 52nd STREET

AMERICA'S FINEST BARBECUE RESTAURANT

Pick-a-rib
INC.

Tiena & Gordon's

ON 52nd ST.
'TWEEN 6TH & 7TH AVE.

PICK
A-RIB
RESTAURANT

CLOSE · COVER · BEFORE · STRIKING

BOB'S BAR-B-Q
INC.

CAFE

JUNCTION
2 & 20
ROLLING PRAIRIE
INDIANA

CLOSE COVER BEFORE STRIKING

Barbecue matchbooks

7

Backyard Bliss

It's hard to say exactly when a cultural trend becomes a fixture of American life, but I have a nominee for one of those moments. On Monday, April 8, 1957, the backyard barbecue became a prime-time TV plot device. That was the night the "Building a Bar-B-Q" episode aired on the CBS situation comedy *I Love Lucy*.

Let's review: Lucy and Ricky have left their New York apartment for a spacious colonial in Westport, Connecticut, their pals Ethel and Fred moving into the guesthouse. As new residents of the suburbs, the four decide to do what any meat-loving Americans with a backyard wanted to do during the 1950s: build a brick barbecue pit. On the day the boys finish the project, Lucy discovers that her wedding ring is missing, and being Lucy, she does something zany. Afraid that she dropped it in the mortar Ricky and Fred had mixed up, she and Ethel frantically disassemble the barbecue pit under cover of darkness. When they still can't find the symbol of her troth in the cement, they rebuild the structure during the wee hours of the morning. When the sun rises, we behold a misshapen brick anomaly that looks like a cross between the Leaning Tower of Pisa and something Salvador Dali might have conjured if he had worked in masonry. Cue the laugh track.

There's a postscript that says something else about the suburbanization of barbecue. The owners of Lucille Ball's childhood home in Celeron, New York, hired a brickmason in 2013 to reconstruct the famous barbecue pit in the backyard. "It was more exciting than a regular barbecue because it was way harder to build," said Jason Sivak, who was used to laying bricks that actually lined up.

OPPOSITE: *Sunset* magazine published the first true barbecue cookbook in 1938. Early editions of *Sunset's Barbecue Book* carried more instructions for building a pit than recipes and were handsomely illustrated with drawings promoting outdoor cooking, California style.

Barbecue went prime time in 1957 as Lucy and Ethel comically reconstructed their husbands' brick pit in *I Love Lucy*.

His handiwork was unveiled at the annual Lucille Ball Comedy Festival, where it was celebrated with a barbecue that featured hot dogs and baked beans. Like a lot of Americans who love to cook outdoors, they didn't realize (or care) that the thought of referring to hot dogs as barbecue would strike many people as a gag itself.

Barbecue was too good a thing to remain the property of southerners, Texans, and people in a few other pockets of the country. During the suburban housing upsurge after World War II, a domesticated version of the old hickory pit spread across the land and became a familiar part of family life in America. It didn't require digging a trench in the yard, only some basic building materials. The movement didn't start in the South or any of the other barbecue heartlands; it started, like so many lifestyle fashions, in California.

The Pacific Coast has its own history of grilling and smoking derived from indigenous peoples, Mexican ranches, and campfire cooking in the cowboy way. One publication married that heritage to home entertaining and has promoted it for more than a century. The Southern Pacific railroad founded *Sunset* magazine in 1898 to tout the West as a tourist destination and as a safe and pleasant place to live. The magazine ran its first barbecue story in 1911 with instructions for a dish that sounds inspired by Mexican barbacoa: Beef a la Californienne, or pit-cooked bulls' heads. Hundreds of grilling articles followed, usually involving more mainstream foods, but magazine recipes are not where *Sunset* made its greatest impact on the evolution of outdoor cooking. That happened in 1938 when the publication brought out what is widely considered the first book exclusively about barbecue.

Sunset's Barbecue Book looks like it was carved from redwood. The early editions are covered front and back with rectangles of grained wood, and they have handsome woodcut illustrations inside continuing the rustic theme. The editors evidently felt a need to introduce the subject to readers because there's an asterisk after the first mention of the word in the title and this explanatory footnote: "The noun 'barbecue' is defined in the dictionary as 'a social entertainment of many people, usually in the open air, at which one or more large animals are roasted or broiled.' Through common usage, however, the word has also come to mean the structure—fireplace or stove—on which any sort of outdoor cooking is done. We use the word this way throughout this book. It seems simpler all around not to argue about it."

Sunset took that part about the structure very seriously. In the 1945 repackaging of the book, the first seventy-one pages were devoted to building and using barbecue pits, in elegantly detailed line drawings complete with curlicues of smoke rising from the chimneys. The recipes and suggested menus take up less than a fourth of the volume. Grilled steaks and seafood dominate the fare, little of which would be called barbecue in Texas or North Carolina.

Bringing out the finest flavor

Season your steak with a skillful hand and a world of flavor comes flooding forth. But be timid with your touch and the taste lacks fullness. Be overly vigorous and you taste the seasoning instead of the flavor. It takes a gift of genius to lure shy flavors from their hiding places. And you sense this gift in the matchless flavor that is yours in every bottle and can of Schlitz...brewed with just the *kiss* of the hops.

Just the KISS of the hops

Copyright 1947, Jos. Schlitz Brewing Co., Milwaukee, Wis.

The Beer that made Milwaukee Famous

In 1947, when this ad for Schlitz beer ran in magazines, backyard barbecue meant cooking on a brick or stone pit.

One of the pioneers, fittingly, was an army veteran from Tulsa, Grant Hastings, who had fantasized about the barbecued ribs back home while serving as an artillery forward observer in combat campaigns in Africa and Europe. After he returned to Oklahoma, he sketched out a plan for the cooker of his dreams and went into business with a partner, Gus Baker. The Hasty-Bake Charcoal Oven came out in 1948; the company, still in business, claims that it was the first grill with wheels, a hood, and a firebox that allowed for cooking over indirect heat.

The Char-Broil Wheelbarrow picnic grill debuted in 1948. An early model is displayed at the W. C. Bradley Museum in Columbus, Georgia.

The people at Char-Broil, in Columbus, Georgia, believe that *they* made the first portable backyard grill. The company traces its history to an ironworks that manufactured cannons for the Confederacy during the Civil War. By the 1940s, its longtime business of making cast-iron farm implements and heaters and stoves was collapsing. Needing a new product, employees designed a charcoal grill that looked like an oil drum cooker mounted on a single wheel. The Char-Broil Wheelbarrow debuted in 1948 and led the old ironworks into a new future in which it became the second biggest seller of grills in America (and the leader in the category of gas grills).

The most familiar early cooker came from Weber-Stephen Products of Palatine, Illinois. George Stephen, a welder at the Weber Brothers Metal Works in Chicago, liked to cook out but wasn't happy with the open brick pit at his home because he couldn't control the heat or the smoke enough for his liking. The metal works made buoys for use on the Great Lakes. Stephen cut one of them in half, attached legs, and added a domed lid with vents to regulate heat and smoke. When George's Barbecue Kettle came out in 1952, it looked a bit homely, like a modified buoy. Redesigned and renamed four years later, the Weber Kettle went on to become such an icon that many people erroneously assume it was the first backyard grill. It remains by far the top-selling charcoal cooker in the world.

Even as Weber and others were conquering the American patio, technology was already changing outdoor cooking. Gas grills had been around since the 1930s but were used mainly in restaurants. The first portable models were marketed in the mid-1950s by CharmGlow Products of Antioch, Ohio; Falcon Manufacturing of Dallas; and the Chicago Combustion Corporation, which later rebranded itself under the more descriptive name LazyMan. Many of the early gas grills were promoted by natural gas suppliers, such as Arkla, the Arkansas Louisiana Gas Company, and were permanent installations hooked up to fixed lines. As gas grills caught on, propane tanks became the dominant fuel source.

One of the curious success stories in backyard cooking is the Big Green Egg. The company's founder, Ed Fisher, grew intrigued with Asian rice cookers—*kamados*—when he was serving overseas with the U.S. Navy. He adapted the concept for a heavy ceramic barbecue grill which more or less named itself because it was big, colored a vivid green, and shaped like an egg. After opening shop in Atlanta during the mid-1970s, the Big Green Egg gathered a cult following who inevitably called themselves Eggheads and inspired several other competitors who make kamado cookers.

Seven decades after the first portable backyard grill was fired up, the variety of outdoor cooking equipment is breathtaking. Barbecuers can chose from inexpensive charcoal grills, propane gas carts, infrared cookers, electric and wood-pellet smokers, built-in outdoor kitchens, trailer-mounted hardwood-fueled rigs, and everything in between, costing anywhere from thirty dollars to thousands. Even with all the choices, humble charcoal and gas grills still command the almost $1.5 billion U.S. market.

In the 1990s, sales of gas models passed charcoal and stayed ahead, taking barbecue a little farther from its hardwood beginnings. Americans respect the past, but convenience usually wins out.

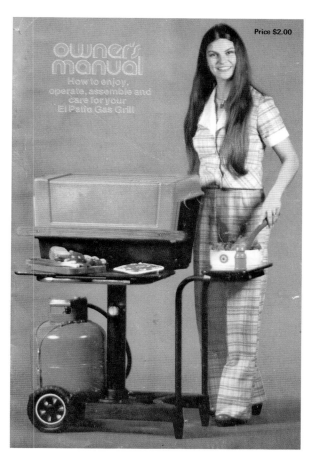

Price $2.00

owner's manual
How to enjoy, operate, assemble and care for your El Patio Gas Grill

This 1977 owner's manual for the El Patio Gas Grill was a symphony of plaids, flared pants, platform shoes, and earth-tone avocado aluminum.

"Men like to barbecue," the comedian Rita Rudner once said. "Men will cook if danger is involved."

Males have long been associated with outdoor cooking, with its fire and tools and specialized equipment, but the stereotypes became especially pronounced when things moved into the backyard. The spread of recreational grilling during the postwar years coincided

Gender stereotyping has always been pronounced in barbecue, especially during the 1950s and '60s. Men were expected to preside over the fire, as shown on the cover of *The He-Man's Cookbook* (1956). Women were expected to make side dishes, so it came as a slight sign of progress when the 1968 Indiana State Fair offered this booklet geared toward women who wanted to cook on gas grills.

with an era when gender roles were at their most traditional and the majority of American women stayed at home managing the household and raising a family. Magazine articles and cookbooks from the 1950s and early '60s made it clear that cooking out was something men did, like mowing the lawn or cleaning the gutters. Grills were usually displayed next to the yard equipment at hardware and department stores, underscoring the presumption that lighting charcoal and scorching steaks was a masculine undertaking.

"Primarily, outdoor cooking is man's work and man-sized menus and portions should be the rule," wrote James Beard in *Cook It Outdoors* (1941), one of the earliest cook-out books. (He also said an old-fashioned barbecue was "as gay as a strawberry festival," but we won't go there.)

More than a decade later, the role-playing had hardened. "It is our belief that the cook should be male," wrote Helen Evans Brown and Philip S. Brown, the married authors of *The Cookout Book* (1961).

"Cooking over charcoal is a man's job and should have no interference from the distaff side of the family. If the man of the house *prefers* to have his wife do the cooking, just skip the idea of doing it outdoors. Nothing makes a man look—and we should think, feel—more hen-pecked than to have his wife officiate at the cookout."

Let's linger on that well-chosen word "officiate." To read the literature of the time or browse the barbecue collectibles online, you'd think that Dad cooking out was akin to a religious rite. There were vestments in the form of funny aprons and chef's hats. There were prayers in the pleadings that the charcoal would ignite. There were worshipful

McCall's sold this sewing pattern for "Mr. and Mrs. Aprons, Hats, and Mitts" in 1957.

FUEL FOR THE FIRE

While humans have been cooking with carbonized wood for eons, the handy modern form of it dates to 1897 when Ellsworth B. A. Zwoyer of Reading, Pennsylvania, received a patent for what he called "lumps of fuel." They're better known as charcoal briquettes.

Zwoyer described his creation as "truncated pyramids with rounded corners and slightly rounded or convex tops." The drawings in his patent application look remarkably similar to what we dump into the grill today. He manufactured charcoal in the early 1900s but was probably ahead of his time because the mass market for outdoor cooking hadn't developed, and the company soon went out of business.

Henry Ford had better timing. In 1919 the industrialist invited his cousin's husband, Edward G. Kingsford, to accompany him, tire maker Harvey Firestone, and inventor Thomas Edison on one of the cushy camping trips they liked to take with their chauffeurs and chef. Kingsford dealt in timberland, and Ford wanted to talk with him about finding a lumber supply for the frames and running boards of his Model Ts. After the two purchased 330,000 acres in the Upper Peninsula of Michigan, Ford built a plant there and established a factory town he named Kingsford.

The milling operation left tons of scrap wood and sawdust. Ford and Kingsford used it to make charcoal, charring the wood and mixing it with cornstarch and other additives that were then compressed into briquets (as they spelled it). Originally sold as Ford Charcoal, the product was renamed Kingsford when it was spun off as a separate company during the 1950s. Kingsford and Match Light (its accelerant-soaked alternative) remain the top-selling charcoal brands, far ahead of their nearest competitor, Royal Oak.

Charcoal was patented in 1897 and used primarily as a heating fuel. It didn't become an outdoor cooking staple until years later, thanks in large part to the Ford Motor Company, which sold its own brand of charcoal and grills. This dealership advertising display dates to about 1940.

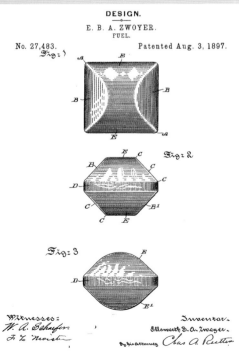

thanks when a platter of meat that had not been cremated somehow emerged from all the sweat and bother.

The 1956 *Better Homes & Gardens Barbecue Book* has an amusing illustration of an idealized cookout that shows how everyone in the family was expected to act. "Dad's the chef," it says, and there he is poking at the steaks. "Sis and Brother kibitz [that's an old barbecue term], pitch in on tasks their size, have the time of their lives." And there they are peering at Dad's steaks, Brother in his Keds and jeans and Sis in her pigtails and white patent leather shoes. "No kitchen chores for Mom," it concludes, and she doesn't look like she's anticipating work, wearing a flowing skirt, a red blouse with puffy sleeves, and a strand of pearls.

But let's get real. There were always kitchen chores for Mom, even on cookout day, because somebody had to make the side dishes and clean up after the Master of Fire and Smoke had performed his ritual.

One indication that barbecue was going national came when it made the cover of the *New Yorker* in 1950. In Perry Barlow's illustration, a uniformed butler pours charcoal for his cigar-studded boss.

The gender stereotyping of the 1950s and '60s was always an exaggerated picture of what was going on around the grill. But exaggerations *are* based on truth. As the years went on, more women cooked outdoors and more men at least stopped acting like it was their God-given responsibility to man the flame. But just because attitudes became less rigid didn't mean that the underlying reality changed. Industry surveys usually find that about two-thirds of the people who cook outdoors are men. Steven Raichlen, the TV grilling guru, once told *Forbes* magazine that he figured men made up 60 to 70 percent of the people who grilled worldwide. "When you grill," he said, "you bring testosterone and fire and sharp instruments together."

Unfortunately, there's no Museum of Backyard Barbecue. Perhaps the phenomenon is too recent and commonplace to merit that sort of consideration. Some manufacturers display cookers that are significant in their history, and a few individuals collect models from one company or another. But there's no one place or person who has documented the passage from earthen trench to brick pit to charcoal and gas grills on wheels.

Which is why I wanted to go see Ed Reilly.

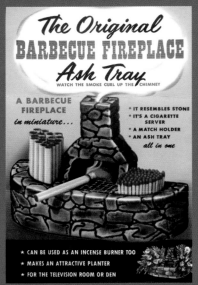

In an early attempt at a cookout playlist, Columbia Records issued *Music for Gracious Living—Barbecue* in 1957. Peter Barclay and His Orchestra performed twelve jazz and easy-listening numbers that seemed right for outdoor entertaining, songs such as "Summer Evening in Santa Cruz."

The Kentucky Tavern ashtray, named for a brand of bourbon, was advertised in magazines and comic books during the 1940s and '50s. The replica barbecue pit sent cigarette smoke up its little chimney.

SIZ charcoal starter, a foam accelerant that resembled shaving cream, offered backyard cooks a supposedly easier way to start a fire in 1959.

Coca-Cola offered this nifty cooking guide in 1965. A revolving wheel shows grilling times for various meats and the back has instructions for building a charcoal fire. It ends with this advice: "And for best results, always remember to keep plenty of ice-cold Coca-Cola to serve at your cookout!"

I met Ed a few years ago when the idea for this book came up. He works for a sales agency in Atlanta as a regional representative for Weber grills and smokers and has taken it upon himself to collect everything that has anything to do with outdoor cooking. We'd meet for lunch, and he'd show me photos of all the antique barbecue gear he was buying and storing at his house an hour out of town, occasionally bringing in a small piece so I could touch it. But whenever I asked to see his repository, he'd shake his head no. "You'd think I was a hoarder. Maybe sometime after I clean up the place."

Scores of Weber Kettles and other cookers occupy the yard at Ed Reilly's house near Atlanta. Reilly, a Weber sales rep, started collecting barbecue artifacts and memorabilia because he couldn't stand to see vintage grills tossed out.

That time finally arrived on an overcast summer day when I pulled into his property in the Appalachian foothills and beheld more grills than I had ever seen in one place that wasn't Home Depot on Memorial Day. They were in the carport, under the deck, in the side yard, out back under the trees—more than three hundred cookers of every make and vintage. "I think all this history is important," he told me, "because America more or less invented backyard entertaining."

Ed started collecting a few years ago when Weber discontinued its red kettle. He'd see them on the side of the road being thrown out and feel a pang, so he'd take them in like so many orphans. He's partial to redheads, as he calls them, because his wife and two children have reddish hair.

After he rescued a teal kettle, he broadened to other colors. Then he began bidding online for old cookers from other makers. He bought Char-Broils and Kenmores and Big Boys and Cook'n Kettles and Royal Chefs and Bernzomatics and Structos and camp stoves from the 1800s and a Ford grill and bag of charcoal from the 1930s.

I wondered how his wife felt about all this documentary clutter.

"I know I can't go on doing this," he said. "I'm running out of room and she's running out of patience."

But he keeps finding things he has to have.

"This is one of my favorites," he said, pausing in front of a GE Partio Cart, a forerunner of the outdoor kitchen from 1960, with an electric

Eisenhower Steak

Shortly after he took office in 1953, President Dwight D. Eisenhower became known not just as the commander of Allied forces in Europe during World War II but as a first-rate commander of the grill. Ike liked to startle guests by throwing steaks directly onto the coals. When he fished them out of the fire, the *Atlanta Constitution*'s Ralph McGill wrote, the steaks looked "all charred and black . . . like the remains of a stubborn stump in a burning of trees at a clearing of new ground." Guests usually glanced around to see whether they could surreptitiously feed their share to a dog or cat, McGill continued. "The President enjoys this moment." Several versions of Eisenhower steak have appeared over the years. They go something like this.

Makes 2–4 servings

2 ribeye or sirloin steaks, 2½ to 3 inches thick
2 teaspoons salt
2 teaspoons freshly ground black pepper
2 teaspoons granulated garlic
1 tablespoon olive oil

Mix dry ingredients in a bowl. Brush the steaks on both sides with olive oil and coat them liberally with the rub mixture. Build a fire with lump charcoal, not briquettes (which contain additives that could leave unwanted flavors, since they'll be touching the meat). When the coals are red hot, place the steaks directly on them and let cook for 10 minutes. Then turn them over with long tongs and cook them another 10 minutes on the other side. When the interior registers 140°F on a meat thermometer, remove the steaks from the coals, brush off any ash on the surface, and let them rest for 10 minutes. Cut the steaks across the grain in half-inch strips. The outside should be deliciously charred and the inside pink and moist.

range, a charcoal barbecue, and a rotisserie all contained in a mobile unit with a sporty turquoise finish. "I read somewhere that President Eisenhower had one."

Ed was right. After they left the White House, Dwight and Mamie Eisenhower had a GE Partio Cart at their second home in Palm Springs, California. I know because the Henry Ford Museum in Dearborn, Michigan, acquired the historic grill in 2011 and put it on display as a high-end example of suburban living. "It's the most fantastic thing you ever saw," the former president was quoting as telling his wife in *Palm Springs Life* magazine.

Ike's grill at the Ford museum—it doesn't get more American than that.

Dwight Eisenhower, shown cooking out in 1953 with former president Herbert Hoover, may have been America's grillingest chief executive. After he left office, Ike enjoyed using the General Electric Partio Cart at his retirement home in Palm Springs, California—a high-end, double-fueled cooker that was marketed to "big wheels," as this 1960 ad puts it.

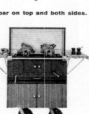

Cornell Chicken

Robert C. Baker may have done more to change the way we eat chicken than anyone but Colonel Sanders. Not only did he create the chicken nugget, but he came up with dozens of new ways to prepare poultry as a professor at Cornell University, where he founded the Institute of Food Science and Marketing. His recipe for grilled chicken, which he devised in the 1950s just as Americans were taking to their backyard grills, became one of the best-known cookout dishes of the era and a staple of upstate New York barbecue. Jim Shahin adapted it for a this modern version in his Smoke Signals column in the *Washington Post*.

Serves 4 to 8

4 chicken quarters

MARINADE

2 large eggs
½ cup canola oil
⅔ cup apple cider vinegar
¼ cup poultry seasoning blend
1 tablespoon kosher salt
½ teaspoon ground
    black pepper

Beat the eggs in a medium-size bowl until blended, then whisk in the oil in a slow, steady stream to form a thickened mixture. Whisk in the vinegar, then the poultry seasoning, salt, and pepper. Pour into a gallon zip-top bag, then add the chicken, massage the pieces, and refrigerate for 4 to 8 hours. Remove the bag of chicken and marinade from the refrigerator and let it sit at room temperature for about an hour.

Prepare the grill for indirect heat. If using a gas grill, turn the heat to high (450 to 500°F). Once the grill is preheated, reduce to medium (375 to 400 degrees). Turn off the burners on one side. If using a charcoal grill, light the charcoal, and when the coals are ready, distribute them to one side of the cooker. For a medium fire, you should be able to hold your hands 6 inches above the coals for 6 seconds.

Place the chicken quarters, skin side up, on the indirect-heat side of the grill; discard the marinade. Close the grill and open its vents halfway. Cook for about 40 minutes or until a digital thermometer inserted into the thickest part of the thigh reads 165°F, turning the chicken as needed. For crispy skin and a little char, move the chicken, skin side down, directly over the coals or flame for the last 3 to 5 minutes.

Barbecue cookbooks proliferated through the 1950s and '60s, as seen in the portfolio over the next few pages. *The Master Chef's Outdoor Grill Cookbook* showed how to barbecue in the rain in 1960. One of the most popular grill makers of the '50s, the Big Boy Manufacturing Company of Burbank, California, issued annual editions of the *Big Boy Barbecue Book*. Duncan Hines, a pioneer of road food restaurant criticism before he became the name on a line of cake mixes, wrote *The Duncan Hines Barbecue Cook Book* in 1955. Beatrice Foods used *Barbecue American Style* to promote its "matchless, self-cleaning" Electro Grills in 1971. The R. J. Reynolds tobacco company put out the *Lazy Man's Cookout Guide* in 1966. Etiquette expert Amy Vanderbilt put her name on a 1965 cookout guide meant to show ladies *How To Entertain out of Doors*.

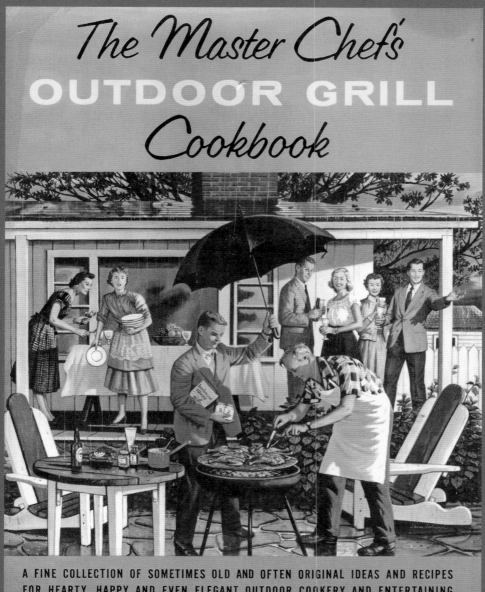

$1.00

Big Boy
BARBECUE BOOK
Shows how easy it is to cook on Spit or Grill

Answers Most Common Questions
- HOW TO BUILD A FIRE
- HOW MUCH CHARCOAL TO USE
- WHEN IS FOOD COOKING
- WHEN IS FOOD DONE
- HOW TO AVOID FLAME-UP

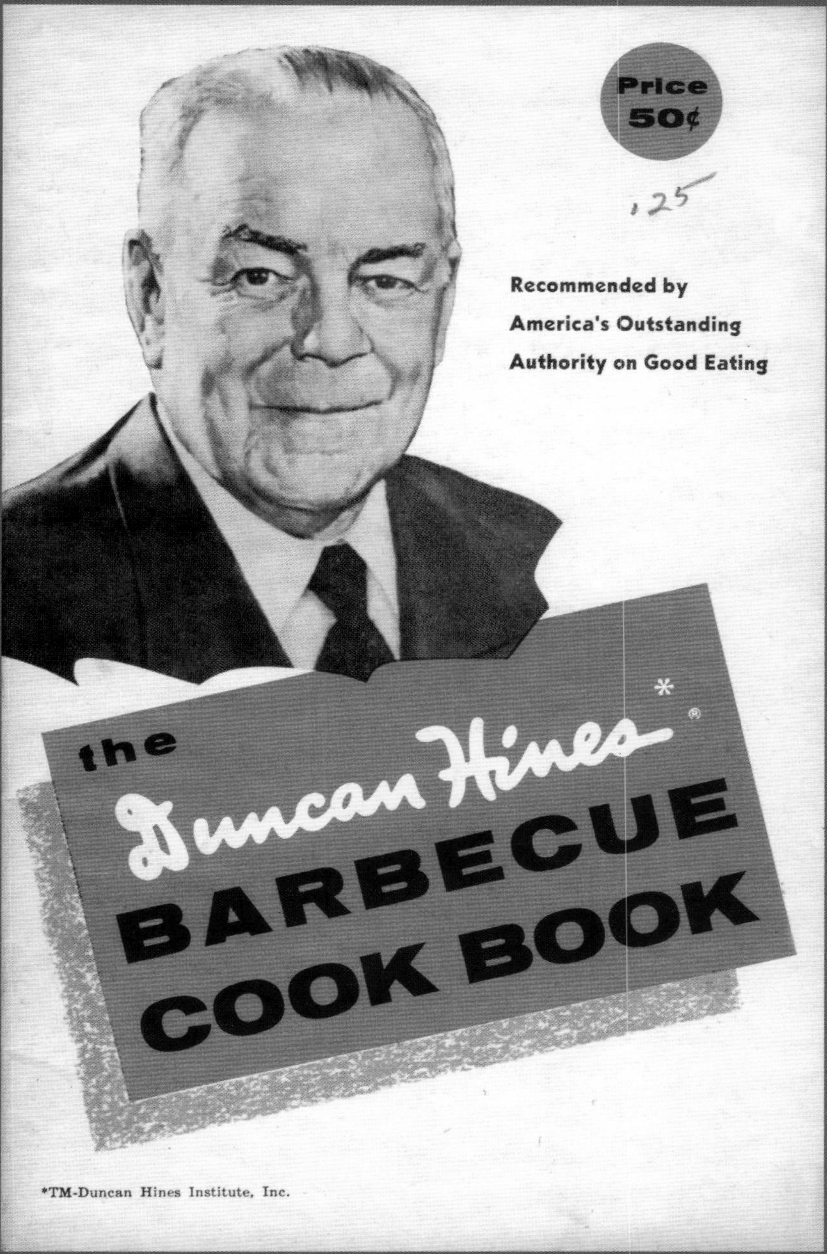

.25

Recommended by
America's Outstanding
Authority on Good Eating

the Duncan Hines* ®
BARBECUE
COOK BOOK

*TM-Duncan Hines Institute, Inc.

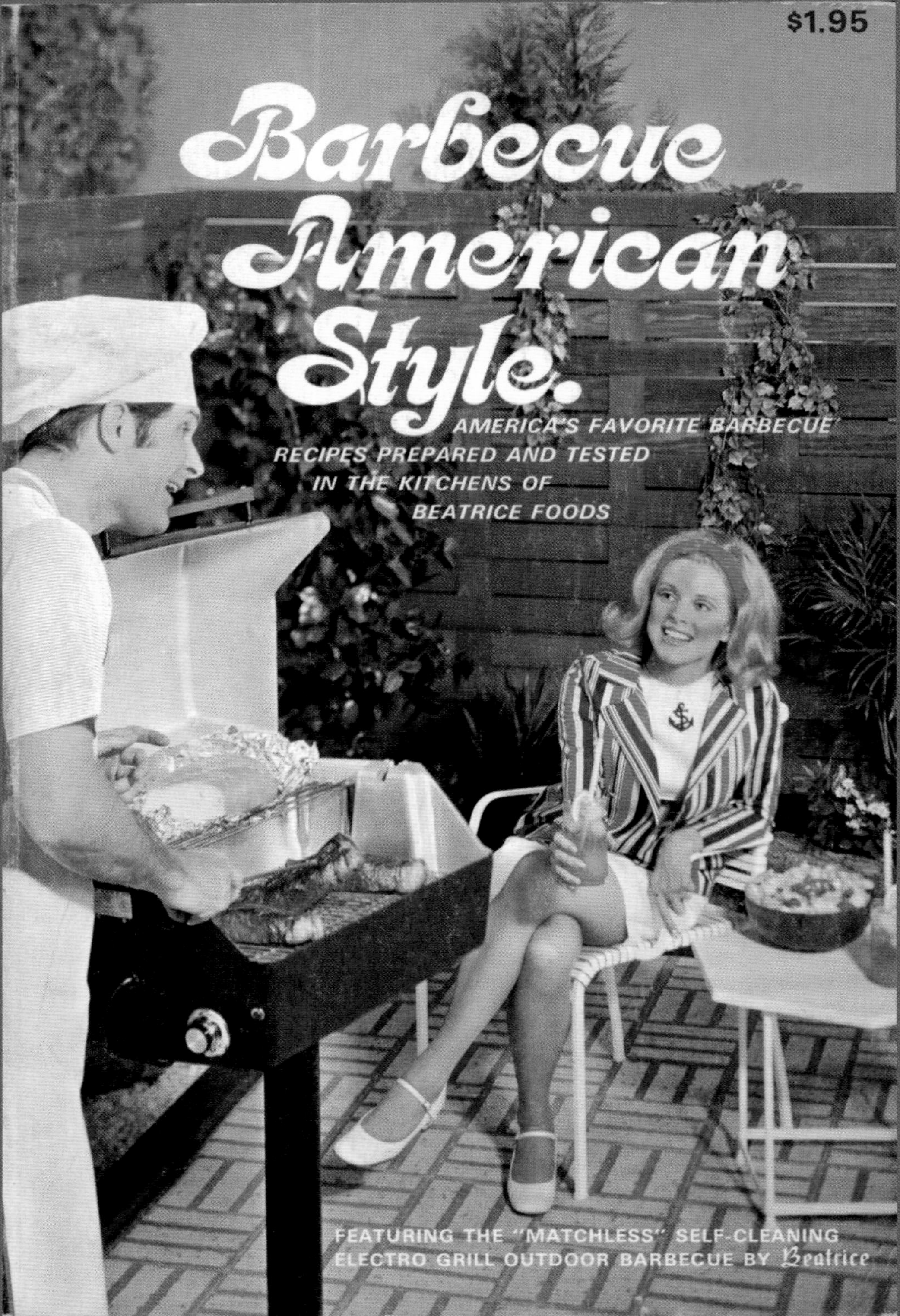

$1.95

Barbecue American Style.

AMERICA'S FAVORITE BARBECUE
RECIPES PREPARED AND TESTED
IN THE KITCHENS OF
BEATRICE FOODS

FEATURING THE "MATCHLESS" SELF-CLEANING
ELECTRO GRILL OUTDOOR BARBECUE BY *Beatrice*

LAZY MAN'S COOKOUT GUIDE

40 PAGES OF RECIPES AND COOKING TIPS FOR EASY-TO-SERVE OUTDOOR MEALS

How to ENTERTAIN *out of doors*

by Lois Dwan

8

The Color of 'cue

The most famous barbecue scene in the movies is probably the Twelve Oaks barbecue near the beginning of *Gone with the Wind*. In the extended sequence, we meet all the major characters—Scarlett, Rhett, Mammy, Ashley, Melanie—as the Wilkes Plantation hosts a barbecue and ball shortly before the outbreak of the Civil War. At one point, Mammy pleads with Scarlett to eat a little something before the celebration so she won't embarrass her family by gorging in front of everyone.

"No!" Scarlett replies sharply. "I'm going to have a good time today and do my eating at the barbecue."

Mammy scowls. "If you don't care what folks says about this family, I does. I told ya and told ya that you can always tell a lady by the way she eat in front of folks like a bird. And I ain't aimin' for you to go to Mr. John Wilkes' and eat like a field hand and gobble like a hog."

I first heard that exchange during the 1960s when I saw the movie as a boy during a rerelease at the Loew's Grand Theatre in Atlanta, the same place it premiered in 1939. As I watched the scene again over the years, especially after I started writing about food, I began to wonder about the barbecue itself. What did they cook? Who did the cooking? How did the producers even know how to stage the antebellum barbecue that defined antebellum barbecues in American popular culture?

They knew because Selznick International Pictures hired someone to research such matters. Wilbur G. Kurtz, an artist and historian in Atlanta, acted as technical advisor on the film, influencing everything

OPPOSITE: Sam's Bar-B-Que in Austin, Texas, serves a history lesson with its smoked meats.

The Twelve Oaks barbecue at the beginning of *Gone with the Wind* might be the most famous barbecue in Hollywood history. Wilbur Kurtz, a technical advisor for the movie, credited "an aged Negro" named Will Hill with providing information about how to stage the scene.

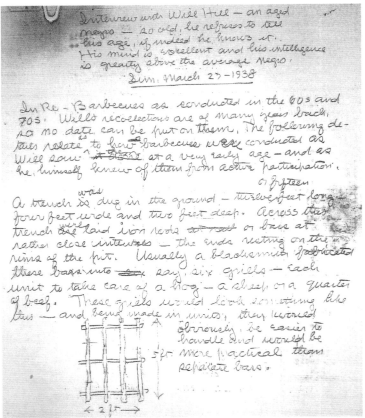

from the way the plantation houses looked to what the slaves wore, often with drawings to show what he meant. Among his papers at the Atlanta History Center is a six-page, handwritten description of how to re-create an Old South barbecue, complete with the dimensions of the trench, diagrams for spacing the rods over the coals, and detailed instructions for cooking and basting the meat. In the first paragraph of the memo, Kurtz discloses that his information is based on a March 1938 interview with Will Hill, "an aged Negro—so old he refuses to tell his age, if indeed he knows it."

Of course. Who else in the late 1930s would have known about the backstage workings of an antebellum barbecue but an elderly Negro who had been there? If you examine the credits for *Gone with the*

Wind on the Internet Movie Database, you'll find Will Hill listed among forty additional crew members as "technical advisor (uncredited)." It's more credit than many people like him ever received.

When I told people I was writing a book about the history of barbecue, one of the comments I often heard went something like this: "Did you find out who invented barbecue? Wasn't it black people?"

Talk about a loaded question.

I usually answered with some learned hemming and hawing that led to my belief that the matter of origin is complicated, that while African Americans are profoundly entwined with the history of barbecue and probably did more than anyone to perfect the art form, you simply can't say that any one ethnic group created a tradition with multiple authors. Black people did not "invent" barbecue, I would conclude; it only seems that way.

Enslaved Africans came to the New World with some knowledge of cooking techniques that prepared them for barbecue. "There are plenty of antecedents in West Africa," says Jessica B. Harris, a culinary historian who has written widely about the continent's cooking and its influence on American food. "They knew how to cook over fire and how to dry and preserve meats with smoke. It was part of the intellectual baggage they brought with them."

Barbecue and slavery took root in America at about the same time, and they spread across the South in tandem. It's clear from contemporary accounts and oral histories that when planters threw a barbecue, slaves did the work: digging the trenches, shoveling the coals, turning and mopping the meat. "It was said that the slaves could barbecue meats the best, and when the whites had barbecues, slaves always did the cooking," wrote Louis Hughes in *Thirty Years a Slave: From Bondage to Freedom*, an 1897 memoir of his life as a bondsman in Mississippi and Tennessee.

Barbecue appears often in slave narratives. Some remembered Fourth of July celebrations when their masters would allow them to take the day off and enjoy themselves with smoked pigs and general frolicking. "Dem days barbecues was de mos' source of amusement for everybody," Wesley Jones, a ninety-seven-year-old former slave in South Carolina, told a Federal Writers' Project interviewer who tried to capture his dialect in the patronizing manner of the time. Jones

The annual barbecue at the F. M. Gay plantation in Eufala, Alabama, was starkly segregated when a photographer for the Federal Writers' Project took this photo in 1936. The picture was part of the America Eats documentary project.

went on to reveal his recipe for the barbecue "sass" he swabbed on the meat all night.

Barbecue also figures in traumatic events associated with bondage. Two slave rebellions in Virginia were plotted at clandestine barbecues. In 1800 a slave named Gabriel hatched a rebellion at a barbecue outside Richmond. Before they could organize their rebel band, they were discovered, captured, and two dozen of them summarily executed. Thirty-one years later, Nat Turner and a small group of slaves in Southhampton County met over barbecued pork and brandy and struck out that night on a bloody insurrection that would claim fifty-three lives—and many more as whites exacted revenge.

TURNING THE MEAT—A GEORGIA BARBECUE AT THE ATLANTA EXPOSITION.
DRAWN BY W. A. ROGERS.—[SEE PAGE 1072.]

Harper's Weekly pictured the barbecue concession at Atlanta's Cotton States and International Exposition on its cover in 1895. The pit was manned almost entirely by black men, while the pit boss was Wilkes County sheriff "Big John" Callaway, one of the leading barbecue men in Georgia.

When freedom finally came, barbecue was there again. On January 1, 1863, the Union troops occupying coastal South Carolina summoned three thousand slaves to Port Royal for barbecue, speeches, and a reading of Abraham Lincoln's Emancipation Proclamation. The guests were serenaded by a military band and served by regimental officers. "They all seemed to enjoy themselves hugely," the *New York Times* reported, "and evidently enjoyed the roast beef more than the oratory."

After the Civil War, freed blacks became even more identified with barbecue in the popular imagination—even if they weren't always given full credit for their contribution. At the Cotton States and International Exposition in Atlanta, for instance, praise for the barbecue concession that fed thousands of visitors to the 1895 fair was heaped on the head cook, "Big John" Calloway, sheriff of Wilkes County, Georgia, a big-bellied, walrus-whiskered lawman who was renowned for his pit prowess. But illustrations in *Harper's Weekly* and other publications show who was really doing the sweat work; in the drawing captioned "Turning the Meat," a crew of black men can be seen flipping the pigs and stirring the pots.

OPPOSITE: "Alabama Barbecue," a breezy ditty packed with food references, was written for the *Cotton Club Parade of 1936*, starring Cab Calloway and Bill "Bojangles" Robinson.

By the late nineteenth century, barbecue had joined the roster of race foods—watermelon, fried chicken, and the like—that were used to stereotype black people. Postcards, advertisements, and editorial cartoons all trafficked in crude racial caricatures. The sheet music of the era, reflecting the interest in minstrel shows, was especially cartoonish, with titles such as "Darktown Barbecue" and "Hog-Town Pig-anninies."

Some of the literature of the day wasn't much better. One of the best-loved writers of the early 1900s, O. Henry, exhibited a regrettable fondness for racial jokes in his short story "The Fourth in Salvador":

"There was a buck coon from Georgia in Salvador who had drifted down there from a busted-up coloured colony that had been started on some possumless land in Mexico. As soon as he heard us say 'barbecue' he wept for joy and groveled on the ground. He dug his trench on the plaza, and got half a beef on the coals for an all-night roast."

White people loved barbecue just as much, but they weren't nearly as apt to be ridiculed for it.

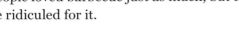

Bobby Seale, the political activist who cofounded the Black Panther Party during the 1960s, published a cookbook years later called *Barbeque'n with Bobby.* Although he had grown up in California, he knew southern barbecue well because his family came from east Texas. When they returned for summer vacations during the 1950s, Seale would help out at the barbecue place his uncle ran in the town of Liberty. His food was so good that white people asked him to enclose a porch so they would have an area to sit down and eat instead of hanging around the parking lot. Seale would serve the black diners on one side of the restaurant and then walk around the corner to serve the white ones, making his uncle's establishment one of the first sort-of integrated places in town.

The irony obviously sunk in. "Being so closely related to the South," Seale wrote in his cookbook, "barbecue was part of segregation and helped defeat it."

Mr. Wesley Jones's Barbecue Mop

One of the best descriptions of antebellum barbecues appears in an oral history given during the 1930s by Wesley Jones, a ninety-seven-year-old man in Union, South Carolina, who had been born into slavery. Culinary historian Michael W. Twitty adapted his instructions for making a barbecue mop in this recipe, which he included in his James Beard Award–winning 2017 memoir *The Cooking Gene.*

4 tablespoons (½ stick) unsalted butter
1 large onion, yellow or white, chopped
2 garlic cloves, minced
1 cup apple cider vinegar
½ cup water
1 tablespoon kosher salt
1 teaspoon coarse black pepper
1 teaspoon red pepper flakes
1 teaspoon dried sage
1 teaspoon dried basil leaves, or 1 tablespoon minced fresh basil
½ teaspoon crushed coriander seed
¼ cup dark brown sugar, or 4 tablespoons molasses

Melt the butter in a large saucepan. Add the onion and garlic and sauté on medium heat until translucent. Turn the heat down slightly and add the remaining ingredients. Allow to cook gently for 30 minutes to 1 hour. To be used as a mop or glaze during the last 15 to 30 minutes of barbecuing and as a dip for cooked meat.

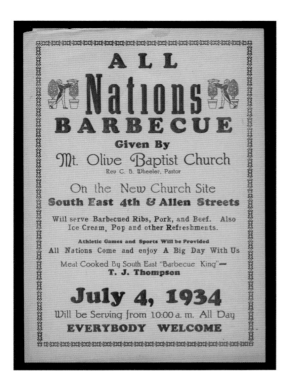

A broadside for a 1934 barbecue at a
Baptist church in Des Moines, Iowa,
where T. J. Thompson, the "South East
Barbecue King," was the big attraction.

There were always barbecue restaurants that blurred the color line. Most of them were black-owned businesses that accommodated white customers. William N. Jones of the *Afro-American* in Baltimore wrote about one in Decatur, Alabama, when he was in the area covering the 1933 trial of the Scottsboro Boys, a scandalous case in which a group of young black men were accused of raping a white woman on the flimsiest of evidence. "You sit in a typical little barbecue restaurant and see white men and women go into the kitchen, stand there and eat barbecue sandwiches. After you have eaten one of these specially treated pork sandwiches, you will understand why these Southern

James Willis of Leonard's Barbecue in Memphis, shown here in the 1980s, was a prototypical African American pitmaster.

whites from the country are willing to reverse the general order of Mr. James Crow and come into a colored eating place."

Occasionally a white-owned barbecue restaurant found ways to treat black customers decently in the dining room. At Abe's Barbecue in Clarksdale, Mississippi, the Lebanese family that has run the eatery since the 1920s proudly talks about the times they served black travelers at the counter over the protest of some of their white regulars.

More commonly, though, white barbecue places allowed blacks only at the back door or the takeout counter. That's the way they did it at Ollie's Barbecue in Birmingham, Alabama, and they saw no reason to change just because there was a new federal law.

When President Lyndon B. Johnson signed the Civil Rights Act of 1964, banning segregation in most public venues, restaurants in the South for the most part grudgingly complied. Some did not. In Atlanta, Lester Maddox closed his fried chicken emporium, the Pickrick, rather than cater to both races, and then parlayed his defiance into a political career that took him to the Georgia governorship.

Ollie McClung wasn't the kind of person who would chase civil rights testers away from his door with an ax handle as Maddox had done. At forty-eight, he was a lay minister in the Cumberland Presbyterian Church and had preached before black congregations. "Many Negroes," he said, "occupy a higher station in the eyes of God than whites do." Still, he didn't think the federal government should tell him how to run his affairs.

Ollie's was located in a mostly black neighborhood on the south side of Birmingham and did a brisk takeout trade with local residents, but only whites were allowed to sit inside. There was a black high school nearby, and McClung feared that the kids might make his place a hangout and run away his white clientele if he desegregated. In September 1964, he filed suit against the Justice Department to challenge the new law. He won a ruling in U.S. district court in Birmingham but lost on appeal that December when the U.S. Supreme Court ruled unanimously that the civil rights act applied to his restaurant because it bought almost half its meat from out-of-state suppliers and was subject to Congress's power to regulate interstate commerce. Rather than close, Ollie's integrated without incident and remained one of Birmingham's favorite barbecue places for decades. After it closed in 2001, the McClungs continued to sell Ollie's barbecue sauce in area groceries.

Ollie McClung of Ollie's Barbecue in Birmingham, Alabama, didn't want to integrate his restaurant and went to court to challenge the Civil Rights Act of 1964.

Another restaurant challenge to the civil rights law came from South Carolina, where Maurice Bessinger ran several barbecue joints around Columbia under the names Piggie Park and Little Joe's Sandwich Shop. Bessinger barred blacks from the dining rooms and

Maurice Bessinger of Maurice's Piggie Park in West Columbia, South Carolina, slapped an image of the Confederate flag on bottles of his mustard sauce and became a lightning rod for controversy.

The Old South Bar-B-Q Ranch, a tourist stop in Clewiston, Florida, mixed southern and western trappings, with plenty of Rebel flags.

was sued in federal court. He lost the case but never quit pressing his cause, running for governor in 1974 as an unapologetic segregationist who made campaign appearances wearing a white suit atop a white horse. He courted controversy again in 2000 when South Carolina decided to remove the Confederate battle flag from the Capitol dome. Bessinger protested by flying the Rebel banner at his nine restaurants and slapping it on the label of Carolina Gold, his widely distributed mustard-based barbecue sauce. The NAACP launched a boycott, while Walmart and other retailers yanked his products from their shelves. In his autobiography, *Defending My Heritage*, he claimed that political correctness had cost him $20 million in sales.

A couple of years before Bessinger died in 2014, my wife and I stopped by his flagship Piggie Park in West Columbia. As we entered the restaurant, we saw a table stacked with religious tracts and political literature attacking civil rights and justifying slavery. A larger-than-life portrait of Bessinger hung on the wall, his white suit resplendent against the crisscross of a Confederate flag. We were seated across from a party of what appeared to be college students—two white, two black—who looked around the place pointing and elbowing one another as if they were on some kind of sociological field trip. I guess they were: a field trip to the past.

Bessinger's family soon took down the flags and turned the page, explaining that they were interested in barbecue, not politics.

Michael W. Twitty was watching a TV show a few years ago when he heard the owner of a South Carolina restaurant suggest that barbecue was created by Native Americans and European settlers, with no mention of black people. Twitty was peeved. Descended from slaves in the Carolinas, the culinary historian believed in his bones that his forebears and people like them had quite a bit to do with the development of barbecue. "I am taken aback by those who would re-assign the culture of barbecue to 'good old boys,'" he wrote in his blog, an early salvo in what would become a campaign to correct what he saw as a whitewashing of memory.

Not long after that post, I drove to Virginia to watch Twitty cook a hog in an open pit at Colonial Williamsburg and talk about the origins of barbecue. It was the hottest day of July, more than a hundred degrees, and he was dripping sweat as he tended the fire and mopped the meat. He wore a white homespun shirt and straw hat in keeping with the reconstructed setting, and he drank water from a dipper instead of a plastic bottle. A muffled ring sounded from the ditty bag slung over his shoulder. "My cell phone," he said, smiling. "We're not supposed to have those."

As Twitty cooked, he told the gathering that barbecue was "co-evolved," that it owed as least as much to the cooking ways of West Africa as to the natives of the Caribbean and the Europeans who encountered them. "Was it invented in the South or in the

Culinary historian Michael Twitty, shown re-creating an antebellum barbecue at Colonial Williamsburg in 2012, drew attention to the unheralded contributions of African American cooks.

islands or in Africa?" he asked. "Yes, no, and maybe. You can't deal with barbecue's roots if you can't deal with complexity."

In other venues, Twitty has been more provocative. In an op-ed column he wrote for the British newspaper the *Guardian*, he accused "bubbas" of appropriating barbecue history. The headline put it plainly: "Barbecue is an American tradition—of enslaved Africans and Native Americans." The article drew more than seven hundred comments, many from people who seemed to resent the suggestion that their grill came with a bag of latent guilt. "In the follow-up story," one reader wrote, "we will learn how toilets are a symbol of oppression in the USA as the pits for latrines were often dug by slaves."

But Twitty was not alone in believing that African Americans have been shortchanged for their contributions to barbecue. Adrian Miller, author of the book *Soul Food*, complained in several guest blogs for the Southern Foodways Alliance that black people were underrepresented in media coverage of barbecue. "Like good barbecue, my annoyance over this subject has been burning like a slow fire, and it hit a flashpoint last year. The Food Network aired *Best in Smoke*—a barbecue competition show that featured six contestants, six assistants, one host, three judges . . . and no black people."

The complexion of the show probably reflected the fact that relatively few African Americans participate in barbecue contests. The organizations that sanction cook-offs have long understood that competitive barbecue appeals to an overwhelmingly white demographic. They've tried to interest black cooks but have met with only limited success. Perhaps it's because of the cost of outfitting a cook-off team or the suspicion many might hold that they would feel out of place. Carolyn Wells, executive director of the Kansas City Barbeque Society, wondered if it's something more elemental. "I've about concluded that black people don't think they have anything to prove when it comes to barbecue."

She might have been onto something. Payne's Bar-B-Q, which makes one of the best chopped pork sandwiches in America, is less than five miles from the park that hosts the Memphis in May barbecue contest. Flora Payne entered once years ago but hasn't returned because she doesn't see the point of trying to win a trophy. "It takes time," she said, "and I've got a restaurant to run."

One of the few African Americans who has found success on the contest circuit is Marlando "Big Moe" Cason of Des Moines, Iowa, an easygoing, cigar-puffing cook who wears extra-large bib overalls to accommodate his 350 pounds. Cason got serious about barbecue

OPPOSITE: Moe Cason of Des Moines, Iowa, was one of the few African American pitmasters to make a name for himself on the barbecue contest circuit.

after he left the navy and started entering contests in 2006. "There were eighty teams at the first one I went to, and I was the only black dude," he remembered. "Same at the next contest and same at the next one. It felt strange to see nothing but white people when you think about how barbecue basically started with slaves."

Cason's barbecue won prizes in more than thirty states, and he became a minor celebrity after he appeared as a contestant and then a judge on the cable TV show *BBQ Pitmasters*. With few exceptions, he felt welcome in the world of competitive barbecue. "I don't see color when I'm competing," he said, "but I do realize that I stand out a little. Sometimes people come up to me and say, 'I'll bet *you* can cook some good barbecue,' and they've never even tasted my food. They're just saying that because I'm black and we're supposed to know about barbecue."

Martin Luther King Jr. really liked barbecue. Taylor Branch, the civil rights historian, once said that as much as King admired Gandhi and his philosophy of nonviolence, he didn't get the Gandhian emphasis on fasting. "He used to joke, 'Gandhi obviously never tasted barbecue.'"

The pages of civil rights history are stained with barbecue sauce. While a few white-owned restaurants resisted desegregation, there were others owned by African Americans who gladly enlisted in the cause. Brenda's Bar-B-Que Pit in Montgomery, Alabama, printed flyers during the bus boycott of 1955–56. Lannie's Bar-B-Q Spot in Selma helped feed the protesters who descended on the city in 1965 to march for voting rights. King knew both eateries, but his favorite barbecue place was much closer to home.

Aleck's Barbecue Heaven was a rib shack in the West End section of Atlanta. Because of its location near Morehouse, Spelman, and other historically black colleges, the modest storefront restaurant functioned as a gathering place for student activists and civil rights leaders. King, who lived nearby and was an old friend of the owner, Ernest Alexander, liked to stop by at night to get a rib sandwich dripping in Aleck's special Comeback Sauce—this despite his wife Coretta's cautions that he should try to go easy on the pork.

"Martin loved those ribs," recalled his colleague Andrew Young, who went on to become a congressman, U.S. ambassador to the United Nations, and mayor of Atlanta. "He'd get them whenever he

had an important speech to write. When he ate ribs, he couldn't just lie down and go to sleep. They'd keep him up all night reading and writing."

By the time Aleck died in 1986, the street out front had been renamed Martin Luther King Jr. Drive. The rib shack closed a few years later, replaced by a Walmart the neighborhood had been lobbying for. One of the things I remember most vividly about the restaurant was the booth in the back where a brooding black-and-white portrait of King looked down from the wall. Pamela Alexander, who ran the business for more than two decades after her father suffered a stroke, was the one who had the picture put up. She had been a civil rights activist in college and deeply respected the man.

When I went to Aleck's, I told her after the place closed, I always shied away from sitting in the King booth because it felt like a shrine.

"It was," she said.

It was a shrine to a man and also, in its way, to the exalted and complicated role barbecue has played in African American culture.

Aleck's Barbecue Heaven on the west side of Atlanta was Martin Luther King Jr.'s favorite barbecue place. After his assassination, the restaurant honored him with a memorial booth, shown here in 1993.

To subscribe, call 404•522•4141

The Atlanta Journal-Constitution | ajc.com
Delivers all day.

SUNDAY, MAY 23, 2010

PARADE

Mmm... Barbecue!

Our Annual Summer Grilling Guide with Chef Bobby Flay— & Homer Simpson

MATT GROENING

9

Of Pits and Poets

What do Mark Twain, Louis Armstrong, John Steinbeck, Eddie Murphy, Tennessee Williams, Zora Neale Hurston, Nat King Cole, Flannery O'Connor, Blind Willie McTell, Ralph Ellison, the Little Rascals, and OutKast have in common? I wish I could say that they all put out their own brand of barbecue sauce (Huck and Jim's Mighty Mississippi Marinade?), but celebrities didn't always do that kind of thing. What they have in common is they are all American artists, and being American, they all slipped a little barbecue into their work. In fact, one of them actually worked at a barbecue place—perhaps the one on this list you would least imagine.

Barbecue has been such an ingrained part of American life for so long that it constantly turns up in our music, literature, painting, photography, film, theater, and television. Sometimes barbecue is the topic, but more often it's only mentioned in passing, adding a splash of verisimilitude to a scene. Other times the word is used metaphorically to refer to something that is most definitely not smoked meat.

Consider this chapter a survey of barbecue and the arts. We'll start with the form of creative expression that has spent more time around the pit than any other.

THE SONG IS 'CUE

The first American composition about barbecue was not a blues tune that you'd hear at some rib joint on the South Side of Chicago. Nor was it a country song that you might find on a jukebox in small-town Texas. The first barbecue music—perhaps the first piece of American

OPPOSITE: Homer Simpson, striking a noble pose on *Parade* magazine in 2010, usually played a barbecue buffoon.

Newspaper ad for
"Pig Meat Blues," a
Paramount "race record"
by Ardell Bragg, 1926.

art of any sort to depict barbecue—was, surprisingly, classical, a genre that does not leap to mind when one thinks of chopped pork and sliced brisket.

Anthony Philip Heinrich immigrated to America from his native Bavaria during the early 1800s and is regarded among music historians as one of the first full-time professional composers in the young republic. Curious about his adopted land, he set out on a journey down the Ohio River in 1817 and settled in a log cabin near Bardstown, Kentucky. He became enthralled with all things rustic and frontier, writing several pieces about nature and Indians and pioneers and slaves. One of his earliest compositions, in 1826, was "A Sylvan Scene of Kentucky, or the Barbecue Divertimento, Comprising the Ploughman's Grand March and the Negro's Banjo Quickstep." A divertimento is a light, entertaining piece usually written for a chamber orchestra. The composition is occasionally performed as a historical novelty, but you're not likely to hear it blaring from loudspeakers at a barbecue festival.

Barbecue found its true soundtrack a century later when blues and jazz recordings flourished during the 1920s and '30s. Quite a few songs have barbecue in the title, but it doesn't take a scholar to figure out that most of them are referring to a different sort of flesh. When Bessie Jackson sang, "I got a sign on my door: Barbecue For Sale," in her 1935 record, "Barbecue Bess," she wasn't talking about pulled pork. Neither was "Big Boy" Teddy Edwards in "Who Did You Give My Barbecue To?" (1934) or Vance Dixon and His Pencils in "Meat Man Pete" (1931) or Memphis Minnie in "Pig Meat on the Line" (1941). More than half the titles in *Barbecue Any Old Time*, a 2011 CD collection of early barbecue songs from Old Hat Records, are unabashedly about sex.

The best-known barbecue recording of all time set the template in 1927. Louis Armstrong's "Struttin' with Some Barbecue," an instrumental written by his wife, Lillian, uses the word in the lingo of the Jazz Age to mean a fine-looking woman. More than a decade later, songwriter Don Raye added lyrics and turned it into a tune that actually seems to be about food:

Mister waiter, if you please,
Another rib or two.
And I'll go strut, strut, struttin',
Struttin' with some barbecue.

To this day, most songs that mention barbecue are not literally about barbecue. No one knows exactly what OutKast, the Atlanta hip hop duo, intended by the title of their 1998 track "Skew It on the Bar-B"—slang dictionaries say the phrase means mixing things up—but it probably didn't involve skewers or grills. Nor was the Animal Liberation Orchestra, a California rock band, talking about ribs in its 2005 song "Barbeque": "Welcome to your barbeque, where we roast all the dreams that never came true."

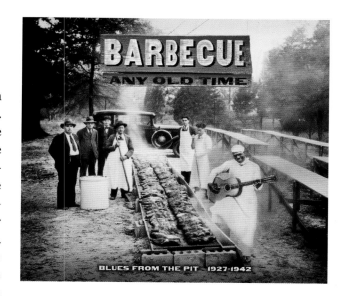

Barbecue Any Old Time, a 2011 collection of barbecue blues. The man with the guitar in the foreground is Barbecue Bob Hicks, who was discovered by a talent scout while working at a barbecue place.

There are songs that really are about barbecue, either the food or the event—recordings such as Nat King Cole's "Riffin' at the Bar-B-Q" (1939), Johnny Horton's "Smokey Joe's Barbecue" (1957), and Clarence "Gatemouth" Brown's "Sheriff's Barbecue" (1975). Two of the best songs celebrating barbecue came, fittingly, out of Memphis and Texas. Wendy Rene, a Memphis soul singer, recorded "Bar-B-Q" in 1964 at Stax, the studio known for Otis Redding and Booker T and the MGs. It's a lip-smacking groove cowritten by guitarist Steve Cropper in which the singer testifies about how much she, her neighbors, and even her pets crave a certain dish:

My poor dog has got a bone,
And he wants some barbecue.
I've got an old gray cat sittin' on the stone,
And he's beggin' for barbecue.

Robert Earl Keen, a Houston country-rock singer, wrote perhaps the most clever song on the subject in his 1994 valentine to smoked meat, "Barbeque." The refrain starts out like a menu scrawled on a chalkboard:

Barbecue sliced beef and bread,
Ribs and sausage and a cold Big Red.
Barbeque makes old ones feel young.
Barbeque makes everybody someone.

A few of the many songs about barbecue (literally or metaphorically):

Animal Liberation Orchestra: "Barbeque" (2005)

Barbecue Bob Hicks: "Barbecue Blues" (1927)

Bessie Jackson: "Barbecue Bess" (1935)

Bo Carter: "Pig Meat Is What I Crave" (1931)

Brownie McGhee: "Barbecue Any Old Time" (1941)

Bucko and Champs: "Australians, Let Us Barbecue!" (2011)

Cary Swinney: "They Don't Serve Barbecue in Hell" (2000)

Elvin Bishop: "Barbecue Boogie" (2010)

Fiddlin' John Carson and Moonshine Kate: "Corn Licker & Barbecue" (1929)

Frank Zappa and the Mothers of Invention: "The Eric Dolphy Memorial Barbecue" (1969)

Frankie "Half Pint" Jackson: "Down at Jaspers Bar-B-Que" (1928)

Hoodoo Rhythm Devils: "The Barbecue of DeVille" (1972)

Ink Spots: "Alabama Barbecue" (1937)

Joe Ely: "BBQ and Foam" (1979)

Jorma Kaukonen: "Barbeque King" (1980)

Juggernaut Jug Band: "Barbecue on Broadway" (2001)

Louis Armstrong: "Struttin' with Some Barbecue" (1927)

Luna: "Cindy Tastes of Barbecue" (2004)

Mannheim Steamroller: "Scotty's Barbecue" (2012)

Marcia Ball: "Peace, Love & BBQ" (2008)

Memphis Minnie: "Pig Meat on the Line" (1941)

OutKast: "Skew It on the Bar-B" (1998)

Paul Desmond: "Samba with Some Barbeque" (1968)

Robert Earl Keen: "Barbeque" (1994)

Tim McGraw: "Something Like That," known by many as the Barbecue Stain Song (1999)

Trent Willmon: "Dixie Rose Deluxe's Honky Tonk, Feed Store, Gun Shop, Used Car, Beer, Bait, BBQ, Barber Shop, Laundromat" (2004)

Wendy Rene: "Bar-B-Q" (1964)

Widespread Panic: "Ribs and Whiskey" (2006)

ZZ Top: "Bar-B-Q" (1972)

Mere lyrics aren't enough for some musicians. A handful of acts have liked the barbecue vibe so much that they made the word part of their stage names. Georgia birthed the rock bands Mighty Fine Slabs, Bar-B-Q Killers, and Sex BBQ; New Orleans spawned the jazz ensemble Kermit Ruffin and the Barbecue Swingers; and Massachusetts gave us the alt-rock group Graveyard BBQ (whose fans are known as BBQ Nation). Farther afield, Britain produced Jimmy Miller and His Barbecues, Canada exported King Kahn & BBQ Show, and Germany generated Dieter Kropp and the Fabulous Barbecue Boys. And then there's Barbecue Bob and the Spareribs, a New Jersey blues outfit whose name recalls the young man who might have been the first recording artist to take on a barbecue moniker.

Bob Hicks was working as a cook at a barbecue drive-in in Atlanta, Tidwell's, when he was discovered by a traveling talent scout in 1927. Signed to Columbia Records, he was rechristened Barbecue Bob and posed for a publicity photo strumming his guitar in a white cook's apron and cap at the restaurant. His first side, "Barbecue Blues," had nothing to do with food but concerned a woman who left him. Barbecue Bob departed himself just four years later, dying of tuberculosis at the age of twenty-nine.

He wasn't the only noted blues singer in Atlanta who plied his trade at a barbecue joint. Blind Willie McTell, whose singing and nimble guitar playing influenced musicians such as Bob Dylan and the Allman Brothers, played for tips from curb-service customers at the Pig 'n Whistle restaurant on Ponce de Leon Avenue. He performed at other Pig 'n Whistles around Georgia and for a time billed himself as Pig 'n Whistle Red.

An ad announcing the opening of a Pig 'n Whistle barbecue drive-in in Atlanta, 1928. There were Pig 'n Whistle chains in Georgia and Tennessee. The one in Georgia was associated with several musicians, including the bluesman Blind Willie McTell.

One more music note: As far as I can tell, Jimi Hendrix never did a song about barbecue, even metaphorically, but he figures in a pretty good barbecue reference. Hendrix, of course, earned notoriety for dousing his Fender Stratocaster with lighter fluid and setting it on fire. "I used to laugh at him because I thought his guitar looked like a piece of barbecue," joked a member of his band, Bobby Womack. In 2008 one of Hendrix's flame-kissed guitars fetched $450,000 at auction, making it almost assuredly the most expensive "barbecue" ever sold.

TICKLING RIBS

When amateur cooks started trying to build fires in their backyard grills, one of the oldest gags in barbecue was born: men blowing themselves up as they set a match to charcoal and lighter fluid. Comics and animated cartoons have been particularly fond of barbecue buffoonery. Donald Duck torched his nephew ducklings on the cover of Disney comics. Spike, the bulldog in the Tom and Jerry cartoons, scorched his face at a cookout in MGM's *Barbecue Brawl*. So did Huckleberry Hound in the 1958 Hanna-Barbera short *Barbeque Hound*, and Popeye's nemesis, Brutus, when he tried to crash a cookout with Olive Oyl in the 1960 cartoon *Barbecue for Two*. The joke was still going strong decades later when Homer Simpson drained a can of starter fluid and ignited a mushroom cloud over Springfield in *The Simpsons*.

Eddie Murphy captured the testosterone-fueled tomfoolery of an annual family cookout in a memorable (and obscene) 1983 comedy bit called "The Barbecue." His know-it-all Uncle Gus comes over and commandeers the grill, ordering others to cut down a tree, chop up some wood, and get two gallons of gas so they can make a fire and eat. After a few drinks, Eddie tells him off.

"Gus, why is the fire so big? . . . You come in here every [bleepin'] year and you burn down my [bleepin'] backyard. Why, Gus? . . . I'm cooking [bleepin'] hamburgers and franks. I'm not cooking a [bleepin'] brontosaurus burger. This ain't the [bleepin'] Flintstones. . . . Look at Charlie standing over there with thirty-degree burns on him."

Ah, yes, *The Flintstones*. We mustn't neglect Fred and Wilma going to the prehistoric drive-in and ordering a slab of dinosaur ribs so large it tips the car over.

Flash forward to the twenty-first century, and cartoon barbecue takes a darker turn. Consider Black Dynamite, an action hero on the

Prehistoric ribs at the drive-in from the opening credits of *The Flintstones*, 1960.

Cartoon Network's *Adult Swim*, who encounters another action hero grilling human beings on a spit. "Mr. T," he says, "you can't go around barbecuing people like they're chicken." Some of the victims are boiling in vats of barbecue sauce, eagerly lapping it up as they stew. They look strangely happy.

THE ART OF BARBECUE

Wine bottles, cheese wedges, and bowls of fruit often appear in European paintings. American artists haven't done nearly as much with their oldest food tradition.

The best barbecue art has been the work of African Americans who portrayed it as an essential part of black life. Raymond Steth, a Philadelphia printmaker with the Works Progress Administration, recalled his childhood on a North Carolina farm in *Southern Barbecue* (1940), a night scene showing several people watching as a whole hog cooks over a pit, their faces glowing in the light of the coals (see p. 28). Jacob Lawrence, one of the best-known black artists of the twentieth century, painted a window full of ribs at a Harlem storefront in *Bar-B-Que* (1942). Archibald Motley, a Chicago artist, completed two paintings called *Barbecue*, one in 1934 and another

Brothers BBQ, a 2017 painting by artist Lucy Hunnicutt, paid homage to Archibald's in Northport, Alabama, and other homespun barbecue places.

in 1960. The latter shows a lively lakeside scene of partying couples arrayed around a brick pit and a heavyset man in a white chef's hat who brandishes his barbecue tools like a band leader with a baton. Margo Humphrey, a Maryland printmaker, created one of the most popular modern barbecue works in *The Last Bar-B-Que* (1989), reimagining the biblical tableau with Jesus and his disciples—all of them black—gathered at a table laden with chicken and watermelon.

In addition to such artists, many fine photographers have been drawn to barbecue as a subject. During the Great Depression, Russell Lee and Marion Post Wolcott documented barbecue joints and community barbecues as part of their fieldwork for the federal Farm Security Administration. In recent decades, noted photographers like Al Clayton and Wyatt McSpadden have focused their cameras on pitmasters and their habitats, finding stark beauty in the back rooms where meat and smoke become barbecue.

Some barbecue places themselves could be seen as works of folk art. While many barbecue restaurants look normal enough with their red-checkered tablecloths, pine paneling, and profusion of pig knickknacks, the genre is notorious for idiosyncrasy: hand-painted signage, thrift-shop furnishings, oddball displays of art and tract literature that reflect the enthusiasms of the owner. One of the most flamboyant examples sits next to the Zell Miller Mountain Parkway in the North Georgia town of Ellijay, where Colonel Poole's Bar-B-Q and Pig Hill of Fame became a roadside attraction. The proprietor, a retired military man, dreamed up the Hill as a promotional device where diners could pay a few bucks to have their names painted on plywood stand-ups of hogs. More than five thousand of them spread across the slope behind the restaurant, looking like a cross between a graveyard and a folk art environment worthy of Howard Finster.

Poole's Bar-B-Q and Pig Hill of Fame in East Ellijay, Georgia, makes for one of the oddest roadside attractions in barbecue. John Baeder painted this view in 1995.

The vernacular architecture of many barbecue restaurants—"sow-haus," as Greg Johnson and Vince Staten called it in their book *Real Barbecue*—adds to the air of do-it-yourself eccentricity. Many old-line barbecue places occupy shacks, cement-block dives, or buildings that were used for something else. Some of the best barbecue in America is served in former gas stations—places like Payne's in Memphis; Southern Soul on St. Simons Island, Georgia; and Joe's Kansas City in Kansas, where the restaurant shares space with a still-functioning Shamrock filling station and convenience store. (*Very* convenient if you overindulge and need a roll of antacids.)

One of the most bizarre adaptive reuses came in Bastrop, Texas, where plans were announced in 2016 to convert the Last Chance Gas Station, the scene of wanton carnage in the slasher movie *The Texas Chainsaw Massacre*, into a restaurant under a sign that says "We Slaughter Barbecue." Plans included a motel catering to lovers of the macabre. "We're going to build a horror barbecue resort," owner Roy Rose said. He didn't say whether the counter help would wear ski masks.

LIGHTS, CAMERA, COOK!

Barbecue has been in the movies for more than a century. The earliest title I've found is a silent comedy from 1915, *At the Bingville Booster's Barbecue*, in which a pompous chef named Indigesto presides over a town barbecue and manages to fall into the pit, where his wife, jealous that he has been flirting with another woman, nearly carves him up with a butcher knife.

There were probably other barbecue films in the silent era, but the next one that shows up in movie databases is a 1924 Our Gang short, *Seein' Things*, starring the Little Rascals. The urchins are trying to hold a "barbercooe," as their kid-lettered sign has it, and things quickly deteriorate into slapstick as they attempt to cook a rooster.

The definitive southern barbecue scene in cinema is no doubt the Twelve Oaks gathering at the beginning of *Gone with the Wind*, which we've already dealt with in the last chapter. The Texas equivalent occurs in *Giant*, the 1956 epic about rancher Bick Benedict (Rock Hudson) and his culture-clashing marriage to Maryland belle Leslie Lynnton (Elizabeth Taylor). At a Lone Star barbecue to celebrate their union, she recoils when she sees a calf's head on the buffet table. "That's real Mexican barbacoa," Bick explains. "Boy, them

SLATHERED WITH WORDS

If "barbecue" suggested sex in twentieth-century popular music, it often signified something gruesome in nineteenth-century literature: cannibalism.

Herman Melville in *Moby-Dick* and Mark Twain in *Roughing It* both used the word to describe the cooking and devouring of missionaries on faraway Pacific islands. "Barbecue" had a similar meaning during the dark days of lynching. In the same vein, Joel Chandler Harris in the Uncle Remus stories had Brer Fox threaten to "bobbycue" Brer Rabbit before getting talked into throwing the clever hare into the briar patch.

More recently, Stephen King, Larry McMurtry, Carson McCullers, Alice Walker, Flannery O'Connor, and Ralph Ellison are among the many novelists who have woven barbecue allusions into their fiction. O'Connor's description of a billboard for a barbecue stand in middle Georgia in *A Good Man Is Hard to Find* is particularly vivid: "TRY RED SAMMY'S FAMOUS BARBECUE, NONE LIKE FAMOUS RED SAMMY'S! RED SAM! THE FAT BOY WITH THE HAPPY LAUGH." Ellison is just as spirited when he introduces the pitmaster in *Juneteenth*: "Mr. Double-Jointed Jackson, the barbecue king, who had come out from Atlanta and was sweating like a Georgia politician on election day . . . supervising sixteen cooks and presiding over the barbecue pits all by hisself."

Our survey of writers and barbecue wouldn't be complete without mentioning three distinguished men of letters who had more intimate connections to the topic than mere words. One of America's Nobel laureate writers, William Faulkner, was known for hosting Fourth of July barbecues at his farm outside Oxford, Mississippi. Another Nobel winner, John Steinbeck, smoked ribs on an oil drum cooker in the tiny courtyard behind his home on the Upper East Side of Manhattan. He was an old hand at such things; years before he wrote *The Grapes of Wrath*, he penned a mock epic poem about his family's barbecues in California. The author identified with pigs so much that he adopted

Das Barbecü, a musical based on Richard Wagner's *Ring Cycle* but set in Texas, opened off-Broadway in 1994.

BARBECUE IN LITERATURE

1689

"Let's barbecue this fat rogue."
—Aphra Behn, *The Widdow Ranter, or,
The History of Bacon in Virginia*

*This play, written in London, contains the
first known literary allusion to barbecue in
the English language.*

1738

"Send me, Gods! a whole Hog barbecued!"
—Alexander Pope, "Imitations of Horace"

1809

Admiral Alpendam arrived without accident in
the Schuylkill, and came upon the enemy just
as they were engaged in a great "barbecue," a
kind of festivity or carouse much practiced in
Merryland.
—Washington Irving, *A History of New York*

1822

Barbecue your whole hogs to your palate,
steep them in shallots, stuff them out with
plantations of the rank and guilty garlic; . . .
—Charles Lamb, "A Dissertation upon
Roast Pig"

1851

I had seen a sailor who had visited that
very island, and he told me that it was the
custom, when a great battle had been gained
there, to barbecue all the slain in the yard or
garden of the victor; and then, one by one,
they were placed in great wooden trenchers,
and garnished round like a pilau, with
breadfruit and cocoanuts; and with some
parsley in their mouths, were sent round with
the victor's compliments to all his friends,
just as though these presents were so many
Christmas turkeys.
—Herman Melville, *Moby-Dick*

1880

"You stuck yourself on that Tar Baby
without so much as an invitation. There you
are and there you'll be until I get my fire
started and my barbeque sauce ready."

"Well, Brer Fox. No doubt about it. You
got me and no point my saying that I would
improve my ways if you spared me."

"No point at all," Brer Fox agreed as he
started gathering kindling for the fire.

"I guess I'm going to be barbeque today.
But getting barbequed is a whole lot better
than getting thrown in the briar patch."
—Julius Lester, in a modern version of
Joel Chandler Harris's Uncle Remus story,
"The Briar Patch"

*In the original, Brer Fox was threatening to
"bobbycue" Brer Rabbit.*

Brer Fox wanted to barbecue Brer Rabbit in an Uncle Remus story from 1880. Floyd Norman, the first African American animator at the Walt Disney studios, rendered the scene more than 125 years later.

1883

"Silver!" they cried. "Barbecue forever! Barbecue for cap'n!"
—Robert Louis Stevenson, *Treasure Island*

Barbecue was another nickname for the pirate sea cook Long John Silver.

1928

All God's chillun got shoes there and fine
    new clothes,
All God's chillun got peace there and
    roastin'-ears,
Hills of barbecue, rivers of pot-licker,
Nobody's got to work there, never no more.
—Stephen Vincent Benét, *John Brown's Body*

1929

"Yes. It's silly, I know. But my people expect me for the Fourth of July. You know, we have an enormous family—hundreds of aunts, cousins, and in-laws. We have a family reunion every year—a great barbecue and picnic. I hate it. But they'd never forgive me if I didn't come."
—Thomas Wolfe, *Look Homeward, Angel*

1932

She had lived such a quiet life, attended so to her own affairs, that she bequeathed to the town in which she had been born and lived and died a foreigner, an outlander, a kind of heritage of astonishment and outrage, for which, even though she had supplied them at last with an emotional barbecue, a Roman holiday almost, they would never forgive her and let her be dead in peace and quiet.
—William Faulkner, *Light in August*

1940

I spotted him in a white barbecue stand tickling wienies with a long fork. He was doing a good business even that early in the year. I had to wait some time to get him alone . . .

"Hot doggies," he chanted. "Nice hot doggies, folks."
—Raymond Chandler, *Farewell, My Lovely*

Hot dogs were considered legitimate barbecue in 1940 Los Angeles.

1946

"By God, it's not too hot for a barbecue. Not if we keep good and away from the fire."

"Troy loves barbecue," said Dabney gravely. It was Tuesday. They had just been away three days, on account of the picking.

But it was too hot for a barbecue, as could be seen by four o'clock, and they took a cold supper.
—Eudora Welty, *Delta Wedding*

1946

He appeared at the bathroom door, braced against the door-jamb, staring at me with a face of sad reproach bedewed with the glitter of cold sweat.

"You needn't look at me like that," I said, "the likker was all right."

"I puked," he said wistfully.

"Well, you didn't invent it. Besides, now you'll be able to eat a great big, hot, juicy, high-powered slab of barbecued hog meat."

He didn't seem to think that that was very funny.
—Robert Penn Warren, *All the King's Men*

1953

They stopped at The Tower for barbecued sandwiches. The Tower was part stucco and part wood filling station and dance hall set in a clearing outside of Timothy. A fat man named Red Sammy Butts ran it and there were signs stuck here and there on the building and for miles up and down the highway saying: TRY RED SAMMY'S FAMOUS BARBECUE. NONE LIKE FAMOUS RED SAMMY'S! RED SAM! THE FAT BOY WITH THE HAPPY LAUGH! A VETERAN! RED SAMMY'S YOUR MAN!
—Flannery O'Connor, "A Good Man Is Hard to Find"

1967

In the ravine my followers, together with the new recruit Jack, had finished the last remnants of their barbecue. Pig bones littered the ground around the ashes of a fire, still smoldering. The five men were reclining amid the cool ferns that rimmed the ravine; they had been talking in soft voices—I heard them as I came down the path with Will—but at my approach they arose and stood silent. . . .
I approached them with an upraised hand and said: "The first shall be last."

"An' de last shall be first," they replied, more or less together.
—William Styron, *The Confessions of Nat Turner*

Turner and his supporters plotted their 1831 slave rebellion at a clandestine barbecue in Virginia.

1969

The charcoal under the ox was turning black, and there was little left of the ox but a skeleton. It had been a good dinner. We had sat on benches in the garden before trestle tables and carried our plates to the barbecue. I had noticed how a stout man who sat beside me refilled his plate four times with huge steaks. "You have a good appetite," I said.

He ate like a good trencherman in a Victorian illustration, with the elbows stuck out and the head well down and a napkin tucked in his collar. He said, "This is nothing. At home I eat eight kilos of beef a day. A man needs strength."
—Graham Greene, *Travels with My Aunt*

1979

"You had some good friends in Ferriday," Mrs. Symes said. "Don't tell me you didn't."

"Not real friends."

"You went to their barbecues all the time."

"The kind of people I know now don't have barbecues, Mama. They stand up alone at nights in small rooms and eat cold weenies. My so-called friends are bums."
—Charles Portis, *The Dog of the South*

1982

They love meat. All the people in this village. Sometimes if you can't get them to do anything any other way, you start to mention meat, either a little piece extra you just happen to have or maybe, if you want them to do something big, you talk about a barbecue. Yes, a barbecue. They remind me of folks at home!
—Alice Walker, *The Color Purple*

Nettie writes to her sister Celie after Nettie has run away from their home in Georgia and gone into missionary work in Africa.

1984

He would stand by the corroding portable barbecue grill, never used now that the kids were gone, and remind himself to wheel it into the garage now that winter was in the air, and never manage to do it, night after night, lifting his face thirstily to that enigmatic miracle arching overhead.
—John Updike, *The Witches of Eastwick*

1992

Two days later he and Rawlins were in the mountains again. They rode hard hazing the wild manadas out of the high valleys and they camped at their old site on the south slope of the Anteojos where they'd camped with Luis and they ate beans and barbecued goat meat wrapped in tortillas and drank black coffee.

We ain't got many more trips up here, have we? said Rawlins.

John Grady shook his head. No, he said. Probably not.
—Cormac McCarthy, *All the Pretty Horses*

1996

I was wide awake, and I could smell Delacroix on me. I thought I might smell him on my skin—barbecue, me and you, stinky, pinky, phew-phew-phew—for a long time to come.
—Stephen King, *The Green Mile*

1997

"You got family in Wichita?"

"Yes. No. Well, my boyfriend does. I'm going to pay his mother a visit."

The guard removed his cap to smooth his crew cut. "That's nice," he said. "Good barbecue in Wichita. Make sure you get you some."

Somewhere in Wichita there probably was very good barbecue, but not in Mrs. Turtle's house. Her house was strictly vegetarian. Nothing with hooves, feathers, shell or scales appeared on her table.
—Toni Morrison, *Paradise*

2000

Maybe the little
bit of meat on ribs
makes for lean eating.
Maybe the pink flesh
is tasteless until you add
onions garlic black
pepper tomatoes
soured apple cider
but survival ain't never been
no crime against nature
or Maker. See, stay alive
in the meantime, laugh
a little harder. Go on
and gnaw that bone clean.
—Honorée Fanonne Jeffers,
"The Gospel of Barbecue"

2001

In the side yard a colored man lifted the top of a barbecue pit made from an oil drum, and the smell of pork lathered in vinegar and pepper drew so much saliva from beneath my tongue I actually drooled onto my blouse.
—Sue Monk Kidd, *The Secret Life of Bees*

2004

Mud Creek, Dreamland, Twixt-n-Tween,
the cue-joints rise through smoke
and glow like roadhouses on Heaven's way.
—Jake Adam York, "United States of Barbecue"

2010

Some call you murder,
shame's step-sister—
then dress you up
& declare you white
& healthy, but you always
come back, sauced, to me.
—Kevin Young, "Ode to Pork"

10
Sauced

Barbecue is more than smoked meat or the gear used to cook it or the social event where it's served. As it grew more popular after World War II, barbecue became a flavor unto itself, reduced to its tangy, smoky, increasingly sweet essence in a bottle of sauce. For millions of Americans, barbecue lives in the condiment aisle of the grocery store, where a glorious confusion of mops, marinades, and sauces beckons in an array of crayon colors. They all contain vinegar and spices, but the consensus stops there. Red or yellow? Hot or mild? Thick or thin? Sweet Baby Ray, it can get overwhelming.

Barbecue purists have a funny attitude about sauce. Many downplay its importance and some disparage it like steak lovers who cringe at the thought of dumping A.1. or Heinz 57 on their ribeyes. If you want to sound knowledgeable at a barbecue joint, request that the sauce be served on the side; they'll think you're a certified contest judge or something. This opinion that the meat should stand on its own is especially pronounced in Texas, where the prevailing sense of pit macho holds that real men use dry rubs. "Barbecue sauce is like a beautiful woman," the singer Lyle Lovett told *Texas Monthly*. "If it's too sweet, it's bound to be hiding something."

Fair enough. Barbecue sauce can overpower meat or mask shortcomings like the proverbial lipstick on a pig. But if sauce is so secondary, why are sauce recipes so closely guarded? Why do cooks tinker with their formulas so much, adding a dab of this, trying a drop of that? Why do so many colorful barbecue stories have to do with some sauce handed down through the generations on a scrap of paper like a marriage license stuck inside a family Bible?

OPPOSITE: Racing legend Richard Petty, a North Carolina native, introduced his own line of barbecue sauce during the 1990s.

I saw how personally people take their barbecue sauces when I hit the road years ago to research *The Ultimate Barbecue Sauce Cookbook*, the first such recipe collection that I know of. I traveled to Texas, Tennessee, Missouri, and the Carolinas to sample sauces and talk with restaurant owners and cook-off teams about their barbecue dressings. At some point in the conversations, I'd gingerly pop the question: *Would you mind sharing your recipe?* I might as well have been asking for their checking account numbers.

A few dismissed me with a dry laugh. Some told me that they'd like to think it over, which was a polite way of saying no. Others cracked that old joke about how they could give me the recipe but then they'd have to kill me. A couple of renowned barbecue places—Sonny Bryan's in Dallas and Lexington No. 1 in North Carolina—actually gave me most of their formula, but withheld key elements to retain plausible deniability. By the time I visited Arthur Bryant's in Kansas City, where a huge bottle of their celebrated sauce sat in the front window like a revered object of folk pottery, I didn't even bother to ask them for the recipe, because I already knew the answer.

Sauce might not be the most important part of cooking barbecue, I came to realize, but it's crucial to the myth and mystery that bathe this most American of foods.

The first barbecue sauce wasn't a sauce as we think of it today but a thin mop used to moisten and flavor the meat as it cooked. Colonial-era accounts of barbecues usually include descriptions of swabbing the pig with a mixture of spices, seasonings, and an acidic liquid like wine or vinegar. Butter, lard, or meat drippings weren't unusual either. Richard Bradley's 1732 recipe in *The Country Housewife* (quoted in chapter 1) is pretty typical: salt, pepper, white wine, lemon peels, sage, cloves.

The few barbecue sauce recipes that turn up in nineteenth-century cookbooks don't deviate much. Mary Randolph gave one of the first ones in *The Virginia Housewife* (1824) in a recipe called "To Barbecue Shote," directing that the young pig be doused with garlic, salt, pepper, red wine, and mushroom catsup. In *Mrs. Hill's New Cook Book*, published in 1867, Annabella P. Hill, a widowed housekeeper in Georgia, offers the sauce her family served at antebellum barbecues: "Melt a half pound of butter; stir it into a large tablespoonful of mustard [powder], half a teaspoonful of red pepper, one of black, salt to taste; add vinegar until the sauce has a strong acid taste."

In the winter of 1909, ads for the first known commercial brand of barbecue sauce appeared in the *Atlanta Constitution*.

Martha McCullough-Williams, a Tennessean who attended many a barbecue during her formative years in the 1800s, remembered a hotter version of the standard Dixie mop in her 1913 memoir/cookbook *Dishes and Beverages of the Old South*. Her father's sauce had vinegar, black pepper, and fiery peppers. "Hot! After eating it one wanted to lie down at the spring-side and let the water of it flow down the mouth," she wrote, recommending cold watermelon as the perfect dessert (and remedy) for inflammatory barbecue sauce.

There may have been commercial barbecue sauces during the late 1800s, but the first brand that can be documented was Georgia Barbecue Sauce, which received a U.S. patent in 1911. Advertisements in the *Atlanta Constitution* picture a bearded black man in an apron tending an open pit, with copy that touts "the finest dressing known to culinary science for Beef, Pork, Mutton, Fish, Oysters, and Game of every kind; roasted, fried or broiled. It is also unequaled for perfecting Brunswick Stew and as dressing for Vegetables." If sushi had been around, they probably would have mentioned that, too.

A handful of other regional brands emerged during the 1920s and '30s. Maull's, a semisweet tomato-based sauce from St. Louis, appeared in 1926 and became synonymous with barbecue and grilling in eastern Missouri. Mrs. Griffin's, a tomato-and-mustard sauce with a heavy dose of vinegar, started out of a home kitchen in Macon, Georgia, in 1935 and is still in production.

Many of the early barbecue sauces came from restaurants. One of the first, Scott's, originated in 1917 at a barbecue place in Goldsboro, North Carolina, where owner Adam Scott claimed that the formula for his spicy vinegar splash came to him in a dream. You can still buy it more than a century later under the old-timey slogan "It's the Best Ye Ever Tasted."

The quintessential barbecue sauce tale may come from another restaurant, McClard's, which started in 1928 as a tourist court, gas station, and diner serving barbecued goat in Hot Springs, Arkansas. A guest who couldn't pay his ten-dollar tab supposedly offered to settle up by divulging his secret recipe for hot barbecue sauce. "That's

A playing card for Maull's, of St. Louis, one of America's oldest barbecue sauce brands.

Scott's of Goldsboro, North Carolina, has sold its peppery vinegar sauce for decades under the slogan "It's the Best Ye Ever Tasted." This ad ran in the Yellow Pages.

Kraft barbecue sauce for sale in 1959 at a Kwik Chek grocery store in Montgomery, Alabama.

my grandfather's story, and we're sticking by it," Joe McClard told me years ago—and four generations of his family have, as their diner became one of the most famous barbecue drive-ins in America. Naturally, that recipe was locked away in a bank vault like an old stock certificate.

Nationally distributed brands didn't come along until the 1940s when Heinz, the Pittsburgh company that had popularized bottled ketchup, started selling its own barbecue sauce. General Foods soon followed suit when it acquired the Open Pit label out of Detroit. Kraft got into the game with Quick-Mix Barbecue Sauce, a packet of seasonings that came with its all-purpose cooking oil but was quickly replaced by a premixed version.

Despite the national brands, barbecue sauce has retained its stubborn regional characteristics. There are still pockets of the country that prefer dressings that other areas regard as endearing peculiarities: the thin black Worcestershire dip that comes with barbecued mutton in Owensboro, Kentucky; the peppery mayonnaise sauce that spread from Big Bob Gibson's in Decatur, Alabama; the hotly debated vinegar sauces that divide North Carolina. West of Raleigh, in Lexington and most of the Piedmont, they use a red splash that gets its color from a dab of ketchup. East of the state capital, ketchup is verboten and the vinegar, salt, and pepper (red and black) speak for themselves. "You don't put red on pork," says Wilber Shirley of Wilber's Barbecue in Goldsboro, North Carolina.

Nowhere do the sauce fiefdoms coexist in such close proximity as South Carolina. Charles Kovacik, a geography professor at the University of South Carolina, received a good deal of press in the 1990s when he and a colleague visited a hundred barbecue places in an effort to identify the state's sauce regions. (Tough research!) They

Alabama White Sauce

Big Bob Gibson's in Decatur, Alabama, has been dipping barbecued chicken in this peppery sauce since the restaurant opened in 1925. Chris Lilly, who married into the family and helps run the business now, gives this recipe for the classic. Lilly has the distinction of heading the only competition barbecue team to win the grand prize at the Memphis in May contest five times.

Makes 2 cups

1¼ cups mayonnaise
¾ cup distilled white vinegar
1 teaspoon fresh lemon juice
1 tablespoon coarsely ground
   black pepper
1 teaspoon sugar
1 teaspoon salt

In a medium bowl, combine all ingredients and mix. Use as a marinade, baste, or dipping sauce. Store in an airtight container in the refrigerator for up to 2 weeks.

Save 5¢ on Andy Griffith's
secret ingredient for tastier barbecues

(Open Pit
Barbecue Sauce)

Pick a hearty Open Pit® flavor: Original Recipe, Hickory Smoke, Mild Garlic. Pour it over your barbecues. Sneak some into the beans. Make it your secret ingredient, too.

Open Pit's extra thick, because it's slow simmered by the chefs at Good Seasons®

Clip this coupon now.
Watch the "Andy Griffith Show" Monday nights on CBS-TV

Andy Griffith peddled Open Pit barbecue sauce while his popular TV show was on the air during the 1960s.

OPPOSITE: French's mustard offered a recipe for "Frenchwise" barbecue sauce in this magazine ad from the early 1950s.

published their results in a paper titled "South Carolina: Epicenter of Southern Barbecue," along with a map showing four distinct sauce territories: tomato, ketchup, vinegar and pepper, and mustard.

That Carolina mustard sauce gets most of the attention. Some historians have traced it to German pioneers, but the sauce didn't really become widespread until the Bessinger family of Columbia and Charleston marketed it at their barbecue restaurants beginning in the 1950s. Maurice Bessinger used to joke that it was God's favorite because it came from the Bible and the parable of the mustard seed. Rien Fertel, in his 2016 book about whole-hog cooking, *The One True Barbecue*, memorably described Carolina mustard sauce as one of the great outliers of American barbecue: "An oddity ostensibly descended

Barbecue
twice as tasty...
with French's

Musts for your barbecue parties are French's golden
rich Mustard and French's savory Worcestershire Sauce.
French's adds a zesty flavor to meats, salads, sandwiches.
No wonder good backyard chefs prefer French's!

FRENCHWISE BARBECUE SAUCE

2 tablespoons butter or
margarine

1 medium onion minced (or
1 tablespoon French's
Onion Flakes)

1 small green pepper minced
(or 1 tablespoon
French's Pepper Flakes)

2 tablespoons brown
sugar

2 tablespoons French's
Prepared Mustard

1 tablespoon French's
Worcestershire Sauce

1 teaspoon salt

¾ cup ketchup

Crush flakes if used. Combine ingredients and
simmer 15 minutes. Yield: 8 servings.

Color Photo by Victor Keppler

Look!

Your Own Handbook on Outdoor Barbecuing!

The R. T. French Co.
1744 Mustard St., Rochester 9, N. Y.

Enclosed is 10¢ in coin. Please send me "Let's Have A Barbecue"—your new booklet of wonderful barbecue recipes and
illustrated plans on how to build outdoor grills.

Name_____

Address_____

City_____State_____

Carolina (and Georgia) Yellow Sauce

Most people associate mustardy barbecue sauces with South Carolina, probably because Columbia restaurateur Maurice Bessinger marketed the best-known brand for years. But mustard sauce has a long history in Georgia as well. Annabella P. Hill, a Georgian, included a mustard sauce in her 1867 collection *Mrs. Hill's Practical Cookery and Receipt Book*, and one of the nation's oldest bottled sauces, Mrs. Griffin's, out of Macon, lists mustard as its first ingredient after water.

Makes 1¾ cups

¾ cup yellow mustard
¾ cup apple cider vinegar
¼ cup brown sugar
1½ tablespoons butter or margarine
2 teaspoons salt
½ tablespoon Worcestershire sauce
1¼ teaspoons ground black pepper
½ teaspoon hot sauce

In a medium saucepan, combine ingredients, stirring to blend. Simmer 30 minutes over low heat.

from another planet, it is the David Bowie of sauces: blond, beautiful, and, though it is way beyond weird, always inexplicably appealing."

Regional differences are fun to talk about, but the larger trend in barbecue sauce preferences has been apparent for years. Most Americans want it red, sweet, and thick. One brand above all has satisfied the common palate.

KC Masterpiece might be the definitive barbecue sauce success story. Rich Davis, a child psychiatrist in Kansas City who liked to cook out on weekends, was eating at a hamburger joint with his wife when he came up with the idea of making a sauce that combined ketchup and mustard. Muschup, as he called it, never took off, but the barbecue sauce he decided to make at the same time, mixing it up in his kitchen with lots of molasses, did much better. KC Masterpiece hit the market in 1977 and quickly became one of the top-selling sauces in the country.

After KC Masterpiece, restaurants and cook-off winners everywhere rushed to peddle their sauces and rubs. One of them was Dave Raymond, a back-yard griller in Chicago who asked his brother, Larry, a trained chef, to come up with a sauce to use in the Mike Royko Rib-off. Royko was a Chicago newspaper columnist and tireless champion of the Windy City, and his rib contest was one of the largest barbecue cook-offs of its time. Raymond's team won the competition in 1982 and started producing a sauce called Sweet Baby Ray's, after the nickname Dave earned for his slick basketball moves as a youngster. From an initial investment of $2,000, it went on to become the number one barbecue sauce in America.

Chicago produced another sauce that became famous in a roundabout way. In the 1960s Argia B. Collins, who ran several barbecue places, started marketing a sweet orange-red topping he called mumbo sauce. Years later, for reasons not fully understood, it won an avid following hundreds of

THE CURIOUS CASE OF LIQUID SMOKE

Most bottled barbecue sauces contain an ingredient listed on the label as "natural smoke flavoring." Sold in the condiment aisle under the name Liquid Smoke, it's the ultimate example of barbecue being distilled to its essence.

Liquid Smoke originated in the 1890s when a Kansas City chemist named Ernest Wright remembered seeing drops of dark liquid running down a smokestack when he was a boy. He devised a way to reproduce that liquid by burning wood in a closed chamber and running the smoke through a condenser. Wright's Condensed Smoke was originally marketed as a shortcut for preserving meats without having to smoke them; users just brushed it on hams like paint. Two competitors from Texas—Figaro and Colgin—began making the product as well, and eventually it became more popular as a flavor additive than as a preservative.

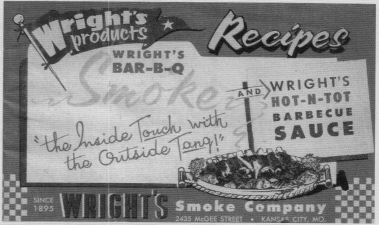

Recipe booklet for Wright's Liquid Smoke and Hot-N-Tot Barbecue Sauce, 1950s.

Liquid Smoke is one of the most controversial substances in barbecue. Many cooks are surprised to learn that it's a natural extract and not an artificial flavoring. Used sparingly, it adds smokiness to sauces and stews, but employed too liberally, it can leave an unpleasant chemical aftertaste. Josh Ozersky, writing in *Eater*, called it "this evil liquid" and compared the flavor to "creosote, formaldehyde, termite mounds, the tears of mendacious orphans, crawlspaces, the acidic musk of old-age homes, guano caves, vinegar, and bad barbecue."

Condensed smoke is found in a wide range of smoke-flavored foods and on the label of almost all the best-selling barbecue sauce brands, from Sweet Baby Ray's and Kraft to Stubb's and KC Masterpiece. In other words, we've all eaten it whether we wanted to or not.

Lay's began selling barbecue potato chips nationally in 1958, around the time a smaller regional brand, Herr's of Lancaster, Pennsylvania, had the same idea. Soon there were barbecue corn chips, barbecue peanuts, and several brands of barbecue crackers with names like Chit Chats and Sociables, one of which ran a silly TV commercial that ear-wormed into my young mind around 1964 because the jingle sounded like a caricature of Beatlemania: "Barb-e-cuuue, barb-e-cuuuuuuue, yeah, yeah, yeah!"

Over the years, barbecue flavorings have been used in almonds, macadamia nuts, sunflower seeds, popcorn, pickles, pork rinds, rice snacks, frozen corn, veggie burgers, even dog food. Eventually Frito-Lay, whose corporate predecessor pioneered barbecue-flavored snacks, introduced regionally specific varieties like Texas Mesquite, Tangy Carolina BBQ, and Sweet Southern Heat.

Some of the food industry's efforts to promote the taste of barbecue during the 1950s and '60s look laughable in retrospect. There's something campy about the old ads for barbecued Spam, Armour Ribs-in-a-Can, Oscar Mayer's Sack of Sauce (hot dogs in a mild barbecue sauce) and Jell-O's Barbecue Salad (a misnamed tomato aspic that didn't even include barbecue sauce).

The most enduring barbecue fabrication was undoubtedly the McRib, a sandwich introduced in 1981 by McDonald's. Created by the same test-kitchen wizard who invented Chicken McNuggets, McRibs are made from ground pork shoulder pressed into a shape that resembles an authentic rib sandwich—but without the bones—served on a bun with onions and copious amounts of barbecue sauce. "Big saucy," McDonald's called it. The sandwich was not a hit at first, but it developed a following as a guilty pleasure and became the butt of jokes on late-night TV and satirical shows like *The Simpsons*. Seeing the marketing possibilities, McDonald's rolled out the McRib in limited releases every few years, like a cult movie, under the slogan: "It's Back!" McRib season usually came in late autumn, during the first chill that farm families know as hog-killing time.

One of the earliest faux-'cue ads was this 1945 display for Texas Style Spam Barbecue. Born of World War II meat shortages, the recipe called for oven-baked Spam "flooded" with barbecue sauce.

At the other end of the food scale, a few high-end chefs experimented with barbecue in nonsavory dishes. At David Chang's Momofuku Milk Bar in New York, they made a barbecue ice cream in 2011. At the Tin Pot Creamery in Palo Alto, California, pastry chef Becky Sunseri created Sweet Barbecue Swirl ice cream in 2016, featuring ribbons of a spicy molasses barbecue sauce set against bits of smoky toffee. "I was expecting something more ketchupy," one sampler told the *Food Republic* website. "It's very salty on the initial taste, which is not unpleasant, with subtle hints of butterscotch. I wonder what it would be like to take a rib and dip it into the ice cream."

If barbecue desserts aren't strange enough, how about products and services that make you smell and feel like barbecue? Que, the first barbecue cologne, came out in 2011, promising a fragrance with "a hint of meat, a dash of spice, and a light finish of summer sweat." Along the same line, the Hotel Crescent Court in Dallas offered a Texas-style barbecue wrap spa treatment, in which patrons would be enveloped in paprika, cayenne pepper, honey, cream, and tomato paste. The only thing missing, mercifully, was smoke.

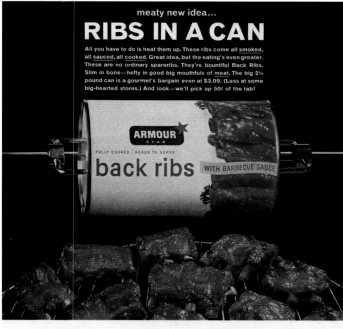

Armour Star advertised canned ribs with "big mouthfuls of *meat*" during the early 1960s.

When I was traveling around barbecue country asking for all those sauce recipes, my most memorable encounter came at Dreamland, the Tuscaloosa rib shack celebrated by sportswriters coming to town to cover University of Alabama football. The restaurant has one of the best barbecue stories you'll ever hear. The founders, John "Big Daddy" Bishop and his wife, Lilly, opened the place in 1958 because, he claimed, the Almighty told him to.

Visit OUR MODERN
Complete FOUNTAIN
FOR TASTY *Castleberry's* pit cooked
BARBECUE SANDWICHES

SOUTHERN BARBECUE

A BIG SANDWICH FOR **30¢**

THEY HIT THE SPOT!
Castleberry's

TEMPTING
Pit Cooked
BARBECUE

SANDWICHES

A Real *Taste* Treat
You'll Never Forget!

Castleberry's
Pit Cooked
BARBECUE
Sandwich
with
TOASTED
BUN **30¢**

Castleberry's
Pit Cooked
BARBECUE
Sandwich
with
TOASTED
BUN **30¢**

Castleberry's TEMPTING
PIT COOKED
BARBECUE PORK
Sandwiches
A Treat
for only **30¢**

Castleberry's
Pit Cooked
BARBECUE
Sandwich
with
TOASTED
BUN **30¢**

Castleberry's
Pit Cooked
BARBECUE
Sandwich
with
TOASTED
BUN **30¢**

try our
Castleberry's
PIT·COOKED
BARBECUE 30¢

John "Big Daddy" Bishop understood the myth and lore of barbecue when he created his tangy tomato barbecue sauce at Dreamland Bar-B-Que in Tuscaloosa, Alabama. He said the sauce came to him in a dream.

I found Big Daddy behind the restaurant sprawled on a lounge chair, looking, true to his nickname, as big as a Crimson Tide offensive tackle. *Men's Journal* magazine had recently tried to crack his red sauce, which was sweet, a tad hot, and so puckery with vinegar that people had been known to take a swig to open their sinuses. I showed him their recipe, and he looked it over with a sneer.

"Shoot, that's a mile off. Ain't none of my stuff in there."

"So what *is* your stuff?" I prodded.

"Dog if I can tell you. God came to me in a dream and gave me this sauce. You see, it's kind of hard for me to talk about."

His daughter, Jeanette, confided that the magazine recipe wasn't far off, so my coauthor on the barbecue sauce cookbook, Susan Puckett, took it as the departure point for developing the recipe we used in our book. People say it's a good approximation of the Dreamland sauce.

When Big Daddy went to that big rib shack in the sky a few years ago, I thought about that day in Tuscaloosa and hoped that he was finally able to thank his creator in person for the divine inspiration.

Yeah, sauce isn't important. It's not important at all.

OPPOSITE: Castleberry's was one of the first companies to turn barbecue into a commodity. It started canning Brunswick stew and sauced meats in Augusta, Georgia, during the 1920s.

11
Trophies as Tall as Steers

In America, almost everything becomes a competition—even something as subjective and unquantifiable as smoking a piece of meat.

Barbecue contests were not the first cooking competitions; state fairs awarded blue ribbons to ladies for their pies and preserves more than a century ago. The rise of backyard entertaining after World War II gave men a socially acceptable way to get into the game.

In 1959, ten years after the inaugural Pillsbury Bake-Off, the Kaiser Aluminum and Chemical Corporation sponsored the first true national barbecue contest. There had been smaller contests before, sponsored by magazines or as part of community gatherings, but this one—the Kaiser Foil Cookout Championship—was on a whole new level. It had written rules, substantial prize money, and lavish promotion. A two-page ad in *Life* magazine announced the contest, inviting cooks to submit recipes using all their "bar-b-tricks." Twenty-five finalists would be chosen from across the country and flown to Hawaii, which had just become the fiftieth state, where they would compete for a $10,000 grand prize and four runner-up prizes of Jeep station wagons.

"FOR MEN ONLY!" the headline proclaimed in red letters. Then, in smaller print: "Men! Enter this great event today! (Gals! See what they do!)."

What they did was barbecue in only a loose sense of the word. The advertising spread included a recipe that seemed a long way from the smoky pits of Carolina; it was for hamburgers moistened with something you'd usually find in a pie filling: Carnation evaporated milk.

OPPOSITE: Mike Mills, a restaurateur in Murphysboro, Illinois, and leader of the Apple City barbecue team, posed with his many trophies in 2014.

Kaiser Aluminum started the first true national barbecue contest in 1959, issuing this booklet of winning recipes in a cover that looked like (what else?) aluminum foil. The contest was held at a resort in Hawaii, a far cry from the down-home atmosphere barbecue competitions would later assume.

The championship took place at the Hilton Hawaiian Village resort on Waikiki beach. *Sports Illustrated* covered the fifth installment, in 1964, probably because writer Percy Knauth had been invited to judge and couldn't turn down a junket to Paradise. His report ran in the back of the magazine, with the chess and bridge columns, and provides a glimpse into the transitional period when many Americans were still figuring out what they could do on a grill.

With his readership in mind, Knauth called the cook-off the World Series of Barbecue and noted with amusement that the actress Joan Crawford was on hand to throw out the first match. Like a sports insider, he explained the intricacies of the scoring system and the strategies contestants employed in their efforts to throw "a no-hit game."

Luau Pork Ambrosia

At the Kaiser Aluminum Cookout Championship, the first national barbecue contest, many entries were examples of what you might call froufrou 'cue—fancy dishes far removed from traditional barbecue. Gail and Annette Erbeck of Mason, Ohio, won the grand prize in 1964 with this recipe, geared toward the cook-off's Hawaii setting.

Serves 6 to 8

1 pork roast, about 5 pounds, chine
    bone removed, tied for roasting
4 (4-ounce) jars strained apricots
    (baby food)
⅔ cup honey
¼ cup fresh lemon juice
¼ cup soy sauce
½ clove garlic, minced
1 small onion, minced
1 cup ginger ale
¼ teaspoon ground ginger
¼ teaspoon ground black pepper
1 (1-pound-13-ounce) can whole
    apricots, unpeeled
1 tablespoon grated lemon rind
¼ cup freshly grated coconut
Parsley sprigs

Place pork in a covered dish. Combine 2 jars strained apricots, honey, lemon juice, soy sauce, garlic, onion, ginger ale, ginger, and pepper. Reserve half the marinade and pour the other half over the pork. Marinate for 4 to 5 hours, turning occasionally.

Line the grill with heavy-duty foil. Light coals and let them burn down until covered with gray ash.

Remove pork from marinade. Place on a spit and cook over low coals for about 3½ hours, until meat registers 185°F inside. During the last half hour, baste frequently with reserved marinade. During the last 5 minutes, spread 1 jar of strained apricots over the roast.

Heat remaining marinade with the last jar of strained apricots to serve as sauce over the meat. Heat the whole apricots and lemon rind together. Remove the roast to a serving platter and garnish with whole apricots, sprinkled with coconut and parsley sprigs.

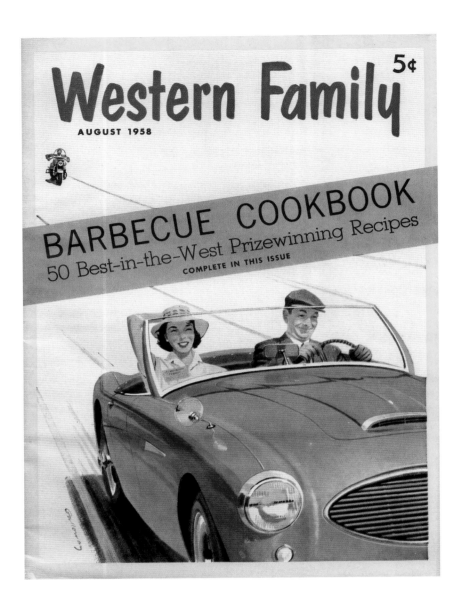

Western Family magazine ran a regional barbecue recipe contest in 1958.

Some of the pitches they hurled toward the judges look like culinary knuckleballs—grilled liver chunks wrapped in bacon and brushed with barbecue sauce, anyone? But the winner seems palatable enough, even if it isn't something a pitmaster would recognize as barbecue. It was a dish called Luau Pork Ambrosia, a roast marinated in apricots, honey, and ginger, and cooked on a spit over coals. The grill was lined with Kaiser aluminum foil, as stipulated in the rules.

The champion, Gail S. Erbeck of Marion, Ohio, used a technique that was not yet common: injecting the pork with a marinade. "He was a dentist," his widow, Annette Erbeck, remembered years later, "so he knew how to give shots."

And so the institution of the barbecue contest was born on a tropical island in the middle of the Pacific. In the coming years, the genre would be refashioned and redefined beyond recognition, exploding in popularity and playing a key role in America's rediscovery of authentic barbecue.

Competitive barbecue, its promoters like to say, has become the fastest growing sport in America. Let's overlook for a moment the question of whether cooking can really be considered a sport. In terms of growth, they might have a point.

There are more than twelve hundred barbecue competitions in the United States today, most of them sanctioned by twenty regional and national organizations such as the Kansas City Barbeque Society, the Memphis Barbecue Network, and the International Barbeque Cookers Association of Texas. There are more competitive barbecue circuits, in fact, than there are minor-league baseball leagues or Football Bowl Subdivision conferences at the top rung of college football. Every weekend, year round, someone is staging a barbecue contest somewhere in America, with scores of them on any given Saturday during the warm months.

THE FIRST COOK-OFF?

In 1870 the *San Francisco Chronicle* carried a brief dispatch headlined "Barbecue at Gilroy." Subhead: "Cashmere Goat vs. Merino Sheep—An Important Issue."

They weren't debating wool. A group of stockmen in the town of Gilroy were trying to settle whether goat or lamb was the superior barbecue meat. Each side chose six judges and selected some fat young kids and lambs to cook. A hundred spectators came out to watch—and feast. In the end, goat won by an 8–4 vote.

J. C. Reid, who covers barbecue for the *Houston Chronicle*, found the story and wrote about it in his blog. He regarded it as more of a throwdown than a real barbecue contest, but still significant. "I've yet to find a reference to any earlier event so closely related to a barbecue cook-off."

In 1978 Bessie Lou Cathey won the first Memphis in May contest, a modest event held in a theater parking lot.

Calvin Trillin wrote about the phenomenon for the *New Yorker* in 1985, just as the contest thing was beginning to take off. He worried that barbecue was going to become the next chili, a humble dish until a group of Texans founded the International Chili Championship in the flyspeck border town of Terlingua in 1967, inspiring innumerable chili cook-offs that gave sweaty men another excuse to argue and brag. "It would hurt to see barbecue go the way of chili—cross over what I now think of as the Chili Line," he wrote. "The fact that just about everything else in the United States seems to have crossed over the Chili Line—labeled and packaged and relentlessly organized and fitted out with promotional T-shirts—doesn't mean that it would hurt any less."

Trillin's tongue-in-cheek concern was well founded. Competitive barbecue crossed the Chili Line like an eighteen-wheeler on a West Texas two-lane and never looked back.

The modern era of barbecue cook-offs began in 1972 when the World Championship Cow Country BBQ Contest started in Uvalde, Texas (Texas again!), followed months later by what is now billed as the World's Oldest Barbeque Cooking Contest in Covington, Tennessee. As you can see, the Federal Trade Commission does not regulate barbecue contest claims. They were soon followed in 1974 by the Houston Livestock Show and Rodeo World Championship Bar-B-Que contest, which grew to become one of the largest competitions and might win an award for longest cook-off name.

But the event that came to define the genre was the Memphis in May World Championship Barbecue Contest. Much of what we associate with barbecue cook-offs—outrageous team names, cartoon pigs running amuck, a party-hearty atmosphere not unlike the beery bonhomie on the infield at a stock-car race—first reared its snout at Memphis in May.

The contest itself was an afterthought. Memphis had customarily celebrated the spring with a Cotton Carnival, a round of galas and private affairs that gave off the distinct magnolia whiff of the Old South. In 1977 a group of younger Memphians launched a new event, the Memphis in May International Festival, that was meant to be more inclusive as it promoted the city's business ambitions with arts and culture and a yearly spotlight on a different nation. One of the planners had competed in the Terlingua chili cook-off and figured a barbecue contest would make a fine addition to the many activities congregating under the festival umbrella.

Memphis in May soon became the prototypical barbecue contest, drawing thousands of people to the banks of the Mississippi River for long weekends of smoke and revelry.

OPPOSITE: The poster from the 2017 edition of Memphis in May says it all.

The first contest, in 1978, was not a big deal. Two dozen contestants entered, their cookers easily contained in a parking lot across from the Orpheum Theater, a movie palace at the foot of Beale Street, the avenue of the blues. The winner, a Mississippi homemaker named Bessie Lou Cathey, pocketed $500 for pork ribs cooked on a portable charcoal grill. Asked for her recipe, she had to admit that her sauce was a doctored version of something she'd found on the shelves at a Piggly Wiggly grocery.

All but one of the entries that year were solo cooks. The only team was a group of young men who called themselves the Redneck Bar-B-Q Express (after the Memphis-based Federal Express). They arrived the night before to smoke a whole hog and invited friends to come by and drink beer and listen to music with them. The impromptu street party mystified festival officials at first. "They asked, 'What are you doing here? The contest doesn't start until tomorrow,'" recalled one of the team members, Pete Gross.

But the festival officials recognized an opportunity when they saw it, and they decided to make the barbecue contest a multiday event in

club for barbecue lovers and contest enthusiasts. "I took the idea to Memphis in May, but they weren't interested," Wells recalled, "so we did it ourselves."

The Kansas City Barbeque Society grew to become the largest barbecue organization in the world. It counts more than twenty thousand members and sanctions more than five hundred contests in the United States, Canada, the Caribbean, Europe, and Australia. The organization celebrated its thirtieth anniversary, in 2016, by moving into spiffy new headquarters in a renovated building in central Kansas City.

The KCBS approached competition cooking a little differently from the folks in Memphis. "I had judged in Memphis and had a lot of fun, but we didn't want our contests to be quite as elaborate as that," Wells explained. "We didn't want multistory cooking clubhouses. We didn't want a category for whole hogs, because those were hard to find around here and expensive. We wanted something that regular people could do without spending a lot of money."

The key difference comes in judging. The Memphis model rewards showmanship and includes a visit to team booths, where the judges are served samples and allowed to inspect the cooking setup—a ritual that can get as mannered as a cotillion. KCBS judging, in contrast, takes place at a central site where trained barbecue experts evaluate the entries in studied silence and record their scores on standardized sheets—a system designed to eliminate all distractions and focus solely on the meat.

Those experts are certified at judging classes the KCBS holds around the country. I enrolled in one before the American Royal contest in Kansas City and saw for myself how seriously these people can take their barbecue. Four dozen of us assembled in a meeting room where a twenty-page handbook waited at each place. I opened to page 7 at random—judging reminders and instructions—and noticed this advice for not influencing other panelists: "Maintain neutral body language. No facial expressions of rapture or disgust. If you need to remove the sample from your mouth, do so inconspicuously into a napkin." I was a little concerned that the last item even had to be addressed.

Our instructor, Mike Lake, who was then president of the KCBS, filled us in on the history of barbecue, its legal definition, competition categories, and all the rules that govern the society's myriad contests. There are lots of rules, especially for presentation. All

The KCBS set strict rules for barbecue judging. When it decided to allow kale as part of the presentation of entries, it was front page news in the society's newspaper, the *BullSheet*.

entries have to be placed in a polystyrene foam container on a bed of lettuce or a handful of other permitted greenery: no fruit, no endive, no red-leaf lettuce.

"Why no red-leaf lettuce?" I asked.

"A long time ago," Lake replied, "someone was suspected of trying to tip off a judge by putting his barbecue on red-leaf lettuce. It was a marker. We don't allow markers because we don't want anyone to know who they're judging. We want to keep it as fair as possible."

(I was amused to read later in the KCBS monthly publication, the *BullSheet*, that certain types of kale were finally being allowed. This momentous news appeared atop the front page under a big green headline: "KALE!")

The class ran another hour and, thankfully, included some practice judging with actual barbecue. Then, at the end of the session, came the moment we had all been waiting for. We stood, raised our hands, and repeated the KCBS oath:

"I do solemnly swear to objectively and subjectively evaluate each barbecue meat that is presented to my eyes, my nose, and my palate. I accept my duty to be an official KCBS certified judge so that truth, justice, excellence in barbecue and the American Way of Life may be strengthened and preserved forever."

Ardie Davis, a barbecue lover and author from the Kansas City area, started a barbecue sauce contest during the 1980s and wrote the judge's oath used at all KCBS contests. He often appears in the guise of an old-time butcher he calls Remus Powers, Ph.B.

The man who wrote those words is Ardie Davis, a KCBS charter member from Kansas who often appears at contests to administer the oath in the guise of a character he calls Remus Powers, PhB. Inspired by the men who worked at old-time meat markets where some of the earliest barbecue was sold commercially, he wears a butcher's apron, a bow tie, a bowler, and a breastplate made of lacquered rib bones. He conceived the getup in 1984 when he founded what was probably the first barbecue sauce contest.

"I was reading Jane and Michael Stern's *RoadFood*," Davis said, "and they had all these barbecue places in there, and it made me real hungry. I couldn't afford to visit all of them like they did, so I asked the barbecue places to send me some of their sauce to get a flavor of what they were doing." With more than one hundred samples from across America, he held the initial Diddy Wa Diddy Barbecue Sauce Contest (named for an old blues song) in his backyard. A few years later, the event became part of the American Royal.

The day after my class, I watched Davis swear in another batch of judges. "I'm proud of that oath," he told me afterward. "Thousands of people take it every year, and it makes them feel official."

It made me feel official—especially a couple of weeks later when the mail brought a silver name plate identifying me as a Certified Barbeque Judge. The first time I pinned it on at a contest, I felt almost like I'd graduated from the police academy.

The rise of the cook-off circuit has affected barbecue like nothing since the popularization of home grilling and smoking during the Baby Boom years. Some people worry that uniform barbecue contests have encouraged homogenization of a tradition cherished for its regional distinctions. There's probably some truth to that; you didn't see much brisket on smokers in the Deep South until KCBS events popped up everywhere. At the same time, competitive cooking has undoubtedly reinvigorated barbecue as thousands of Americans have gone from backyard cooks to dedicated hobbyists, bringing a wider awareness of classic pit practices at a time when they were waning. Some of the winners of those tall trophies have gone so far as to open restaurants and catering businesses, accounting for some of the best new barbecue places in America.

Barbecue-themed street signs on the grounds of the Big Pig Jig contest in Vienna, Georgia, 2017.

They're in almost every state. In Kansas City, Joe and Joy Stehney started a cooking team and enjoyed it so much they opened one of the city's most-recommended barbecue restaurants, Joe's Kansas City. In Savannah, Georgia, Wiley and Janet McCrary used their cook-off expertise at Wiley's Championship BBQ. In Des Moines, Iowa, Darren and Sherry Warth won a bunch of prizes and parlayed their triumphs into three locations of Smokey D's BBQ.

One of the first to build a barbecue empire from contest success was Mike Mills, a former dental technician in Murphysboro, Illinois, near the southern tip of the state. In 1985 he bought a restaurant there, the 17th Street Bar & Grill, and helped launch a barbecue

Some of the hundreds of barbecue contest pins collected by Joe and Carlene Phelps, cofounders of the *National Barbecue News*, a magazine and website out of Douglas, Georgia.

contest to promote the town. He formed a cooking team, Apple City Barbecue, and won the grand prize at Memphis in May in only his sixth competition—and then won it twice more over the next four years, becoming the first three-peat. Mills opened additional barbecue places in Illinois and in Las Vegas, consulted on a high-profile barbecue restaurant in Manhattan called Blue Smoke (with Danny Meyer of Union Square Cafe), and started a barbecue consulting business with his daughter, Amy Mills, who cowrote their cookbook about it all, *Peace, Love and Barbecue.*

When Mills started winning contests in the early 1990s, the only media covering barbecue exclusively were two monthly publications: the KCBS's *BullSheet* and the *National Barbecue News*, a magazine founded by two couples in the South Georgia town of Douglas, Don and Frances Gillis and Joe and Carlene Phelps. Now run by their son Kell Phelps, the *News* is primarily a website—although it still uses an old-school logo showing a cartoon porker with a press card stuck in his fedora as he scribbles away in a notepad.

It was just a matter of time until competition barbecue attracted the attention of TV producers. After the *Iron Chef* series brought the concept of dueling cooks to U.S. audiences in 2005, several reality shows built around barbecue cook-offs began to appear on the Food Network, the Travel Channel, and other venues. The most popular was *BBQ Pitmasters*, which debuted on TLC in 2009 and continued for seven seasons under different formats on the Destination America channel. The show helped publicize a new generation of barbecue celebrities who appeared as judges and occasionally as contestants, almost all of them drawn from the world of barbecue contests.

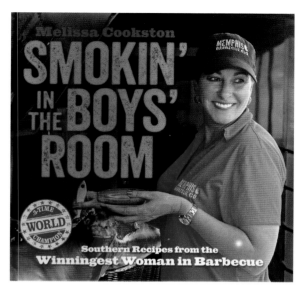

"We're the ones they put on TV," said the KCBS's Wells. "We're the colorful characters, the hams who play to the camera, the people who have the cooking secrets that they'd have to kill you if they were revealed."

Among the new stars was Tuffy Stone, a caterer in Virginia who won some of barbecue's highest prizes as leader of the Cool Smoke cooking team, opening a chain of Q Barbecue restaurants in Richmond. Another was Melissa Cookston, a Memphis in May champion from northern Mississippi who started several Memphis Barbecue Company restaurants and billed herself as the winningest woman in barbecue, calling her 2014 cookbook *Smokin' in the Boys Room*.

But the biggest star of barbecue TV—the only one to appear on every season of *BBQ Pitmasters* and its successor, *BBQ Pit Wars*—was Myron Mixon, head of the Jack's Old South cooking team, four-time grand champions of Memphis in May and winners of hundreds of other contests. With his white mane and beard, usually set off against a black shirt, he looked like he was playing a character: the pitmaster you either admire for being so good or hate for being so cocky. As he began one of his books, *Smokin'*: "I am Myron Mixon, from Unadilla, Georgia, and I am the baddest barbecuing bastard there has ever been."

Told by one interviewer in 2010 that some people found his competitiveness off-putting, Mixon replied bluntly, "Well they can kiss my ass is what they can do."

Good thing they don't give trophies for barbecue congeniality.

Competition barbecue teams are dominated by men. Melissa Cookston of Mississippi regularly beats the boys and has parlayed her success into a career as a restaurateur and cookbook author.

The Houston Livestock and Rodeo Show Barbecue Contest is one of the four biggest competitions, along with Memphis in May, Jack Daniel's, and the American Royal in Kansas City.

You won't see a pig in the logo for the Hava NaGrilla Kosher BBQ Contest in Philadelphia, one of the biggest such competitions in America.

Almost forty years after her husband won the Kaiser Foil Cookout Championship in Hawaii, Annette Erbeck got a chance to see how barbecue contests had evolved when the two of them drove from their home near Cincinnati to the Jack Daniel's World Championship Invitational Barbecue in Lynchburg, Tennessee. She was amazed. In Hawaii, the atmosphere around the Kaiser contest was pure '60s resort swank, down to the pink Jeeps that ferried contestants and their families around Waikiki. In Tennessee, the scene was more like a down-home tailgate party. "There were all these mobile homes with rigs behind them," she remembered. "It was nice, but it certainly was different."

The Erbecks went to The Jack in 2001 because they had won a barbecue sauce contest sponsored by the distillery. The prize: an expenses-paid trip to the championship, one of the most prestigious events on the barbecue calendar. By then the couple were veterans of cooking contests. Annette had been a finalist in the Pillsbury Bake-off three times and had won the National Beef Cookoff and the Pineapple Cooking Classic (bagging another free trip to Hawaii).

Barbecue festivals like the Big Apple Barbecue Block Party in New York have spread across America. Dinosaur Barbecue, a chain that started in upstate New York, is a frequent presence at the event, which draws renowned pitmasters and more than a hundred thousand barbecue lovers to Lower Manhattan every June.

The Jack Daniel's World Championship Invitational, held every October in Lynchburg, Tennessee, is considered one of the most prestigious contests. Its annual posters are prized barbecue collectibles.

Cooking teams are known for choosing colorful names. More of them involve pigs than cows because, well, pigs are funnier. Some of the best:

Swine Lake Ballet	R2-BQ	
MasterBasters	Ribbed for Your Pleasure	
Yabba Dabba Que	Rub Me Tender, Rub Me Sweet	
Church of Swinetology	Hoggy Bottom Boys	
The Pig Lebowski	Aporkalypse Now	
Limp Brisket	Shigs-in-Pit	

Her husband, Gail, had gotten quite a ride from his win in the Kaiser cook-off, appearing on Art Linkletter's TV program and the game show *To Tell the Truth*.

After Gail died in 2004, Annette thought it was finally time to tell the truth about their triumph in the first national barbecue contest. She had been keeping a secret for decades: While her husband was indeed an accomplished barbecuer, the winning recipe, Luau Pork Ambrosia, was not his brainchild. It was hers.

"There were several women there who admitted that they had come up with their husband's recipe," she said, "but we couldn't say anything because of the rules. The contest was just for men. I wouldn't be surprised if there were more of us in the closet who haven't come out yet."

Barbecue, it turns out, was a coed sport from the beginning.

12
A World of Barbecue

In November 2008, two mobile food operations opened for business in Los Angeles. Each called itself barbecue, but they didn't mean the same thing by it.

Neil "Bigmista" Strawder fit the conventional definition. He bought his first smoker to compete in cook-offs and enjoyed it so much that he and his wife, Phyllis, got a portable rig and started selling at the Watts Farmers Market and other venues. They offered classic fare like ribs, brisket, and pork butt, and threw in a few baubles like "pig candy," thick bacon covered in brown sugar and spices and smoked to a caramelized finish. Bigmista's Barbecue was such a hit that they soon opened two fixed-site locations, and its energetic namesake appeared as a contestant on the *BBQ Pitmasters* TV series.

The same month that cooking rig appeared at the farmers market, the Kogi BBQ Taco truck rolled out on the streets of La La Land. The man behind it, Roy Choi, was a Korean-born, California-raised chef who had attended the Culinary Institute of America and worked in ritzy hotel kitchens. He drew on his experiences to create the Korean barbecue taco, a trilateral mixtape of flavors that consisted of a Mexican corn tortilla filled with Korean short-rib beef barbecue, salsa, and California coleslaw. The tacos proved so popular that they touched off a national craze for food trucks and landed Choi a book deal and cinematic immortality as the inspiration for the 2014 movie *Chef.*

Both success stories were built on something their authors called barbecue. The fact that the concept could be that universal—and

OPPOSITE: People around the globe are interested in American-style barbecue. When Korede Alimi won the 2017 Brothers of the Grill contest in Nigeria, his prize was a trip to the Jack Daniel's Invitational in Tennessee.

In Los Angeles, Kogi Korean barbecue taco trucks have attracted a large following by melding foods from both sides of the Pacific.

that malleable—shows how far America's oldest food has come and where it might be going.

When you think about it, barbecue is like rock 'n' roll.

Rock 'n' roll once referred to a specific type of music, but it was so widely and enthusiastically embraced that it came to mean almost any youthful-sounding tune with a good beat and a hint of rebellion. Barbecue once stood for something specific as well—low and slow, over woodsmoke—and it still does to traditionalists. But let's face it: to the world at large, the word now means almost anything cooked on a grill or a smoker, or perhaps only doused with barbecue sauce, as long as it's fun and informal and tastes good. You know, as long as it rocks.

In this ecumenical spirit of culinary globalism, many Americans have taken an avid interest in other interpretations of barbecue around the world. Today's backyard cook is far more likely than earlier generations to know about Jamaican jerk, Asian satay, South American churrasco, Mediterranean souvlaki, Nigerian suya, or any number of other foods that involve smoke and fire. The most visible barbecue TV personality of the past twenty years, Steven Raichlen, has made a career out of exploring international grilling for U.S.

audiences. One of the best-selling of his many cookbooks was his 2010 travelogue *Planet Barbecue!*

It wasn't that long ago that the only barbecue in America—if you were in a part of America that had it—was the barbecue that was native to your region. If you couldn't find brisket in Carolina and couldn't find pulled pork in Texas, you certainly couldn't find Argentinian *asado* beef.

One of the first foreign cuisines in the United States with barbecue-like dishes was Chinese. Back in the 1930s, Victor Bergeron, a tavern owner in Oakland, California, noticed the wood-fired cookers used to make Cantonese *char siu* pork in the local Chinatown. He had an Americanized version built and used it in his next venture, Trader Vic's, the Polynesian restaurant chain that brought us Mai Tais and tiki torches, and still serves *char siu* pork and Chinese barbecued spareribs.

That sort of cultural synthesis set a pattern. If Americans see something that reminds them of barbecue, that's what it's called, whether it is or isn't. Korean barbecue is the name we (or was it Korean restaurants?) gave to *gogigui*, roasted meats cooked on charcoal grills. Mongolian barbecue is a stir-fried beef dish created in Taiwan that bears no resemblance to actual Mongolian cooking—or to American barbecue. Hawaiian barbecue is what people on the mainland call kalua pig, the pork they cook in buried pits at a luau.

There's a restaurant called Waikikie Hawaiian BBQ near my house in Atlanta. It dawned on me how diverse barbecue was getting when I drove out for dinner one night a few years ago and passed the Hawaiian place and three Korean barbecue restaurants before I came to a regular old southern barbecue joint. If you live in a metropolis like Los Angeles, the melange is more dramatic; in the Yellow Pages, almost half the barbecue places listed there are Asian or Hawaiian.

The husband-and-wife team of Jiyeon Lee and Cody Taylor have combined Korean and southern flavors to great acclaim at Heirloom Market BBQ in Atlanta.

Occasionally, barbecue styles meld in one kitchen. One of the happiest examples is Heirloom Market BBQ in Atlanta, where they make a spicy pork sandwich that represents an East-West marriage of flavors, literally and figuratively.

Cody Taylor and Jiyeon Lee, the husband and wife who own the place, met while they were working in the kitchen of a fine-dining establishment. He's a southerner, a self-described "hillbilly chef," who

OPPOSITE: This heroic
2010 poster promoted
Australia Day, the
national holiday marking
the settling of the
country.

societies have organized in Germany and the United Kingdom.
Barbecue contests like the ones in North America have sprung up
in France, Austria, Italy, the Netherlands, and other nations—some
of them sanctioned by the Kansas City Barbeque Society, others
by fledgling European bodies like the Ireland-based World BBQ
Association.

More international cook-off teams are traveling to the States, too.
Almost a quarter of the entries at the Jack Daniel's invitational contest in Tennessee come from overseas. Foreign teams
also cook at the other major contests: Memphis in May,
the American Royal in Kansas City, and the Houston
Livestock Show and Rodeo.

One British restaurant chain, Red's True BBQ,
blogged about its experiences as a visiting team at
the 2016 Houston cook-off. A group of employees
made the journey as part of an annual pilgrimage to
the American barbecue heartland, this time including stops at Alabama favorites like Dreamland and
Big Bob Gibson's. They posted about every stop,
sounding like European blues groupies hitting the
Mississippi Delta, as they snapped pictures of their
food and took selfies with pitmasters. In Houston,
they were introduced to the crowd along with another
British team and one from Japan, all of them roundly
applauded, and then got down to cooking. "All in all,
we came 24th out of 144 in brisket, and 98th overall
out of 430 teams," they wrote. "Not bad for a set of
drunk Brits hey!"

Some countries have a pronounced barbecue culture of their own and don't necessarily need to emu-
late America's. Australia, for instance. Aussies love to
throw just about anything on the barbie (they ought to
trademark that phrase) and have their own barbecue

In South Africa, Jan
Braai promotes *braai*—
the Afrikaans word for
grilling—as a way of
unifying a country still
mending after decades
of racial division and
repression.

TV shows, barbecue equipment makers, barbecue personalities, and
barbecue contests. Many Americans would consider what they do
grilling, but what are semantics among friends?

South Africans also have an indigenous barbecue tradition: *braai*,
the Afrikaans word for grill. They cook anything from sausage and
steak to seafood and vegetables over hardwood embers—no gas or
charcoal—but the food only begins to explain the appeal of braai to a
people still healing from long years of ethnic conflict.

One of the most conspicuous examples of Asia influencing American barbecue is the Big Green Egg. The popular cooker started when a U.S. serviceman adapted Asian rice cookers for smoking. Thousands of fans gather each fall at Stone Mountain Park in Georgia for a grilling festival called the Eggtoberfest.

Lechón, or barbecued suckling pig, is a revered dish in former Spanish colonies worldwide, especially in the Philippines, as shown in this early 1900s postcard.

California Barbecued Oysters

These are essentially grilled oysters anointed with barbecue sauce. As anyone knows who has encountered them driving along the coast north of San Francisco, they are *so* delicious. From *The Ultimate Barbecue Sauce Cookbook*.

Makes enough for 3 dozen oysters

BARBECUE SAUCE

¾ cup ketchup
1 tablespoon Worcestershire sauce
Juice of 1 lemon
1 teaspoon Dijon mustard
Several dashes hot pepper sauce

GARLIC-WINE SAUCE

4 tablespoons (½ stick) butter
1 tablespoon minced garlic
¼ cup white wine

In a small bowl, combine the barbecue sauce ingredients. In a small saucepan, combine the butter and garlic and heat until the butter melts. Then stir in the wine. Place 3 dozen oysters on the half shell on a hot grill and add a teaspoon of barbecue sauce to each. When the sauce bubbles and the oysters begin to curl, add a teaspoon of garlic-wine sauce to each. Remove from the grill and eat immediately.

Archbishop Desmond Tutu, the Nobel Peace Prize–winning anti-apartheid activist, endorsed a campaign to create a National Braai Day in the hope of promoting South African unity over a grill. "We have, what, eleven official languages? But only one word for this wonderful institution—braai," he said in a promotional video. "It has fantastic potential to bind us together."

Tutu noted at one news conference that a T-bone steak sizzling over the fire looked remarkably similar to the shape of Africa.

The man who dreamed up the braai campaign, Jan Scannell a/k/a Jan Braai, was a South African who had worked in New York and seen the way Americans from every walk of life came together over their grills on the Fourth of July. He envisioned something similar for his homeland.

Barbecue, it seems, is about so much more than food.

A few years ago at the Southern Foodways Alliance symposium at the University of Mississippi, I heard a Vietnamese American novelist

Memphis Barbecue Spaghetti

Nowadays you can find barbecue nachos, barbecue tacos, and barbecue-stuffed potatoes from coast to coast. All this tasty cross-breeding started in Memphis with barbecue pizza and barbecue spaghetti. The latter is a specialty of the Bar-B-Q Shop, one of the city's favorite barbecue restaurants, from which this recipe is adapted.

Makes 6 to 8 servings

1 pound thick spaghetti
1 cup chopped onions
¾ cup chopped green peppers
2 garlic cloves, minced
½ cup cooking oil
1 pint sweet, tangy tomato-based barbecue sauce (the Bar-B-Q Shop recommends their Dancing Pigs Original Bar-B-Q Sauce)
1 cup sugar
Dash of liquid smoke (optional)
Dash of salt
1 pound barbecued pork, pulled

In a large skillet, sauté the onions and peppers in the oil until they are tender and the onions are translucent. Add the garlic, barbecue sauce, sugar, liquid smoke if using, and salt, and simmer over low heat for another 20 minutes. Meanwhile, bring a pot of water to a boil. Add the pasta and cook according to directions. While the spaghetti is cooking, add the pulled pork to the skillet and let it warm with the sauce. Drain the pasta and serve it in individual bowls or plates, with the sauce and meat spooned over it.

named Monique Truong read an open love letter she had written to a barbecue place in North Carolina. It was funny and touching, and provided an unexpected expression of how a person could find comfort and meaning in something she had once considered alien.

Truong was only seven when her family fled Vietnam after the fall of Saigon in 1975. They were allowed into the United States as political refugees and sponsored by a family in Boiling Springs, North Carolina, in the Blue Ridge foothills west of Charlotte. They lived fifteen minutes away from the town of Shelby, home of Red Bridges Barbecue Lodge, one of the state's great Piedmont-style pits.

People in that part of North Carolina loved Bridges, but Truong was apprehensive about the restaurant. She was having a hard time fitting in at school, where some classmates called her "Jap" or "Chink," and she imagined that they had learned that casual intolerance from their parents, who might be there eating barbecue. She didn't visit

BARBECUE, LOOSELY SPEAKING

Some terrific dishes called barbecue aren't really barbecue:

Barbecued shrimp. In this New Orleans classic, originated by Pascal's Manale restaurant, shrimp are baked in a garlicky sauce loaded with spices that can turn reddish in the oven, resembling barbecue sauce.

Barbecued oysters. Grilled oysters with a dash of barbecue sauce added to the half shell. A specialty of the northern California coast.

Barbecue pizza. A cheese pizza topped with pulled pork, first served at Coletta's in Memphis. Barbecue pizza appears in numerous varieties and has inspired other add-on dishes like barbecue nachos, barbecue tater tots, barbecue-stuffed jalapeños, and barbecue salads.

Barbecue spaghetti. Another Memphis novelty that comes with barbecue sauce instead of marinara or barbecued pork instead of bolognese.

Eric Vernon, proprietor of the Bar-B-Q Shop in Memphis, with one of his signature dishes: barbecue spaghetti.

Pit beef. It's a Baltimore thing: big hunks of round grilled on a very hot charcoal fire and sliced thin for sandwiches. Bob Creager, owner of Chaps Pit Beef, told *Baltimore* magazine that after Guy Fieri referred to it as barbecue during a Food Network segment, the restaurant received "nasty messages that I should be ashamed of myself for calling it barbecue. Most of the time, I ignore it, but after a while I started responding, saying, 'Dude, I called it 'pit beef.'"

Barbecued salmon. In the Pacific Northwest, natives were smoking fish over alder wood long before Lewis and Clark showed up. The settlers who followed, familiar with pig roasts, called it barbecued salmon or planked salmon, after a cooking method that calls for the fish to be smoked over the coals on soaked planks of wood. They smoke fish in the East as well—planked shad in the mid-Atlantic and smoked mullet on the Gulf Coast—but few people there would refer to it as barbecue.

Spiedie. No one actually calls this barbecue, but it's part of the extended family. Originated in Binghamton, New York, it's a sandwich of Italian bread filled with marinated chunks of meat grilled on skewers. The name probably comes from the Italian word for skewer or spit, *spiedo*.

China: A woman eating grilled squid in Xining.

the eatery until years later, as an adult, when she decided that she belonged at Bridges as much as anyone. Something about the restaurant spoke to her. Maybe it was just the barbecue. "Vietnamese people honor the pig," she said. Maybe it was the mysterious sauce, which she tried to replicate in her own kitchen. Or maybe it was the marvelous retro look of the place, with its teal vinyl booths and the tall neon sign out front that looks like a 1950s motel marquee. Whatever it was, going to Bridges made her feel full and happy and somehow more at home.

At the end of her open letter, Truong disclosed that she had included a barely fictionalized depiction of the barbecue place in her second novel, *Bitter in the Mouth*. "It's a story about tasting and claiming a home in the American South," she said.

Truong's letter was reprinted as a travel piece in the *Washington Post*. Looking over the comments online, I saw the usual nostalgic reveries and good-natured jabbing about which Carolina barbecue style was better. And then I noticed this from someone identified as Ronjaboy:

"Nobody ever wrote an article like this to broccoli."

Well said. Barbecue, whatever you think it is or isn't, is the kind of food that gets love letters—even if you've had to learn it like a new language.

OPPOSITE: Cameroon: A street vendor grilling meats in Bamenda.

Argentina: A man cooking *asado* meats in a food court in Mendoza.

Israel: A makeshift barbecue by the side of the road.

Russia: A couple cooking shashlik—a version of shish kebab—in Bashkortostan.

Epilogue

People have always worried that barbecue—real, pit-cooked, honest-to-God barbecue—was going to fade away. If you love something, it's natural to wonder whether it will always be there. I've wondered.

As I began researching this book, one of Atlanta's oldest and most beloved barbecue places, Harold's, closed after several years of decline. Harold's was on the south side in an industrial section near the General Motors assembly plant where my father and brother worked. It drew blue-collar and white-collar customers of every stripe—cops and lawyers, line workers and accountants, plumbers and reporters—who loved its sliced pork, cracklin' cornbread, and Brunswick stew. Harold's might not have had the best barbecue in town, but it had an everyman appeal and a knotty-pine ambience that captured for me the spirit of barbecue. When CNN called to interview me about the barbecue sauce cookbook I coauthored, I suggested we meet at Harold's because I thought it would make the perfect backdrop. It was what a barbecue joint was supposed to look like.

And then Harold died.

The family of Harold Hembree, who had opened the place in 1947, carried on gamely for a while, but I knew the fire was dying when I stopped by for lunch one day and didn't see any wood stacked out back. It was like learning that a favorite uncle was terminally ill.

Running a barbecue place is hard work, and I'm not sure I'd want to do it. I remember seeing an episode of the TV show *Dirty Jobs* in which the host, Mike Rowe, cleaned out the pit and chimney at Old Clinton Barbecue in Gray, Georgia, near Macon. "The best barbecue

OPPOSITE: Few barbecue places last for generations. Harold's, for sixty-five years one of the most beloved barbecue joints in Atlanta, became a ghost pit in 2012.

225

in Georgia comes from the dirtiest smoker I've ever seen," he said, and then elbowed into the grease and soot like a stable boy mucking out a horse's stall. I can see why barbecue dynasties are hard to perpetuate.

So it was with Harold's. The restaurant finally gave up the ghost in 2012.

Four years after the business closed, I visited the vacant building with a couple of colleagues from the Atlanta History Center who were scouting artifacts for the exhibition that inspired this book. The new property owner, who hoped that someone would reopen it as a restaurant, met us at the front entrance—or at least we could hear him on the other side as he backed out screws with an electric drill. He had the doorway boarded up like a house in a hurricane to keep out intruders.

When he finished removing the plywood and we stepped inside, a musty dampness enveloped us. It was sad. Part of the ceiling had collapsed, dropping tufts of insulation that looked like scraps of white bread. The floor tiles were loose from water damage, the result of copper thieves stripping the fixtures. The knotty-pine paneling was there, but it was mildewed in places. I noticed a religious message slapped on one wall: "God Has Time To Listen If You Have Time To Pray." We came to a tomblike chamber where we could see only with a flashlight. It was the heart of what Harold's had been—the barbecue pit—and it still smelled like smoke.

Standing there in the gloom, I thought about another time I had gone to Harold's. The 1994 Super Bowl was coming to Atlanta, and the newspaper where I worked wanted to give visitors recommendations for finding barbecue not too far afield from the Georgia Dome. I mentioned Harold's and a couple of other respected elders: the Auburn Avenue Rib Shack and Aleck's Barbecue Heaven, Martin Luther King Jr.'s favorite. Now it occurred to me that they were all closed, a generation of barbecue passed away.

I'm telling you all this because something hopeful has happened over the years when we lost those landmarks. A new generation of barbecue has risen. Cook-off champions have opened commercial pits. Classically trained chefs have devoted themselves to the art of fire and smoke. Cooks from other countries and cuisines have brought new

ideas about barbecuing to American kitchens. For every Harold's or Aleck's that has become a fond memory, three new barbecue places have opened in my hometown. I would dare say that Atlanta has more good barbecue now than ever before, and I know the same goes for scores of other cities.

Any way you look at it, barbecue has never been more popular.

You can see it in the continued enthusiasm for barbecue contests. You can see it in the proliferation of barbecue TV shows and barbecue books. You can see it in the condiment aisle at the grocery store, where barbecue sauces and rubs jostle for attention. You can see it in the sales of backyard barbecue equipment, which slowly climb year after year.

And you can certainly see it in the number of barbecue restaurants. There are more than fourteen thousand in the United States

Rodney Scott of South Carolina rose to prominence as one of a new breed of barbecue traditionalists. In 2018 the James Beard Foundation named him the best chef in the Southeast, one of only two barbecue men to win such an honor. The first was Aaron Franklin of Franklin Barbecue in Austin, Texas.

At Scott's Barbecue,
it still starts with
hardwood burning down
in a metal barrel.

JANUARY 22, 1956 — The AMERICAN WEEKLY — BOSTON ADVERTISER

THIS IS YOUR FUTURE

A whole issue devoted to the fascinating
facts about the way you'll soon be living

today. According to CHD Expert, a Chicago company that analyzes the food service industry, barbecue weathered the Great Recession that began in 2008 better than most dining categories, adding new locations every year during the worst of the downturn. Barbecue still represents only a small portion of the nation's restaurants—barely 5 percent—and it's still greatly underrepresented outside the South and Southwest, so there's plenty of room to expand.

What's more, some of those new restaurants have built themselves around the old ways of cooking. The artisan barbecue places in Texas have received ample attention, but the same rediscovery of craft is happening elsewhere. Places that smoke whole hogs, the original American barbecue, have staged a comeback and can be found in six states now. You can find whole hog barbecue in Brooklyn and Atlanta and Asheville and Charleston, where Rodney Scott, a pitmaster of such fundamentalist fervor that he cuts his own wood, became in 2018 the second barbecue man to win a regional award for best chef from the James Beard Foundation.

If the outlook for barbecue shows such promise, why would the loss of one timeworn barbecue place in Atlanta put me in a blue mood?

Barbecue lovers have a tendency to romanticize the object of our affection. We cherish the old places that embody the heritage and want them to remain exactly as they are. We want them to cook on hardwood. We want them to warm the sandwich buns on that little brazier behind the counter like they always have. We even want them to keep that faded photo on the wall of some local TV news celebrity that most of us have forgotten. We don't want them to change.

But they do. Places close and places open. Tastes shift and new dishes come along. Traditions evolve or they calcify. So it is with barbecue. All we can do is respect and remember as we refine and improve.

I love the history of barbecue, but I think I'm going to love its future even more.

Saying grace before a
barbecue in Pie Town,
New Mexico, 1940.

SOURCE NOTES

One of the challenges of writing about barbecue is that very few barbecue people wrote about what they were doing in the early days. It was folk food. Political barbecues and barbecues at large public gatherings made the newspapers, but those articles rarely tell us much about what was on the pit or how it was cooked or who did the cooking.

Things have certainly changed. Starting in the 1980s, barbecue books and barbecue coverage in the media took off, providing an embarrassment of riches for anyone researching the subject.

Before I get into particulars, let me mention two sources that stand above others in writing this book. Robert F. Moss's *Barbecue: The History of an American Institution*, published by University of Alabama Press in 2010, was the first true history of the topic. The Charleston, South Carolina, culinary historian went on to become barbecue editor for *Southern Living* magazine.

The other essential source is the Southern Foodways Alliance, part of the Center for the Study of Southern Culture at the University of Mississippi. I was working for the *Atlanta Journal-Constitution* in 1999 when the late, great food writer John Egerton phoned and asked me to attend an organizational meeting for the SFA in Birmingham, Alabama. There were fifty of us there, and we agreed that documenting the region's foodways would be the most important job for the new undertaking. Under the leadership of director John T. Edge, the SFA has conducted more than one hundred oral histories with pitmasters and barbecue people in ten states, all readily accessible on its website www.southernfoodways.org—and there are many more about other foods. What a valuable resource.

Introduction

An account of George Washington at the Capitol cornerstone ceremony can be found in *Glenn Brown's History of the United States Capitol*, edited by William B. Bushong (United States Capitol Preservation Commission, 2007). The magazine article that featured my grandfather and his Georgia barbecue was "Dixie's Most Disputed Dish" by Rufus Jarman in the *Saturday Evening Post*, July 3, 1954. Bob Auchmutey cooked barbecue and Brunswick stew for all sorts of gatherings from the 1930s through the 1950s. In the diary my father kept during his days at Berry College, he mentions ten public barbecues his daddy oversaw, including one for the sheriff's department on July 4, 1941—"& he got $16.85 for it too—wow!"

Chapter 1. The Smoke of a Distant Shore

Columbus's introduction to barbecued iguana is described in Andrés Bernáldez's *History of the Catholic Sovereigns* (Argonaut Press, 1930) and in Samuel Eliot Morison's *Admiral of the Ocean Sea* (Little, Brown, 1942).

Andrew Warnes analyzes the etymology and connotations of the word "barbecue" in his provocative *Savage Barbecue* (University of Georgia Press, 2008). John Shelton Reed traces early uses of the term in "There's a Word for It—the Origins of Barbecue," an essay in the Winter 2007 issue of the journal *Southern Cultures*. I corresponded with Julian Granberry, coauthor of *Languages of the Pre-Columbian Antilles* (University of Alabama Press, 1993), about the Taino origins of the word.

Charles M. Hudson follows Hernando de Soto's expedition through the Southeast in *Knights of Spain, Warriors of the Sun* (University of Georgia Press, 1997). The first use of *barbacoa* in English comes from Richard Hakluyt's *The Worthye and Famous History of the Travailes, Discovery & Conquest of that Great Continent of Terra Florida* (1611), a translation of a Spanish account. Miles Harvey portrays Jacques Le Moyne, his early illustrations of Indians, and his association with John White and Theodor de Bry in *Painter in a Savage Land: The Strange Saga of the First European Artist in North America* (Random House, 2008). White's illustrations are collected in *America 1585: The Complete Drawings of John White* (University of North Carolina Press, 1984).

Chapter 2. The Cradle

All three states with claims to being the cradle of American barbecue have books that assert their importance. In *Virginia Barbecue: A History* (History Press, 2016), Joseph R. Haynes gives a detailed account of barbecue in the Tidewater region and shoots down a few myths. In *A History of*

South Carolina Barbeque (History Press, 2013), Lake E. High Jr. argues that his state deserves more credit for shaping American barbecue. The Tar Heel State weighs in with *Holy Smoke: The Big Book of North Carolina Barbecue* by John Shelton Reed and Dale Volberg Reed, with William McKinney (University of North Carolina Press, 2008). Bob Garner covered much of the same turf a decade earlier in *North Carolina Barbecue: Flavored by Time* (John F. Blair, 1996).

Barbecue Presbyterian Church lovingly documents its history. A former pastor, the Reverend James MacKenzie, wrote an ode to the church meant to be sung to the tune of "O Tannenbaum." Would it be sacrilegious to think of it as an anthem for Carolina pulled pork?

> O Barbecue, Old Barbecue,
> You've trusted God and found Him true.
> With open heart and open door,
> You've stood two hundred years and more,
> And many on that golden shore
> Are thankful for you, Barbecue.
> O Barbecue, Old Barbecue,
> You've trusted God and found Him true.

John Shelton Reed wrote a post about the Wilmington barbecue "tea party" for the University of North Carolina Press in 2016. Daniel Vaughn investigated the incident and added important details in his TMBBQ blog for *Texas Monthly.*

Mark Essig examined our complicated relationship with pork in *Lesser Beasts: A Snout-to-Tail History of the Humble Pig* (Basic Books, 2015). In *The Kentucky Barbecue Book* (University Press of Kentucky, 2013), Wes Berry surveyed burgoo, mutton, and other barbecue specialities of that state.

I interviewed Sam Jones at the Skylight Inn in Ayden. I also relied on Rien Fertel's tour of whole-hog cooking, *The One True Barbecue* (Touchstone, 2016), and on an article about Jones opening his own restaurant in the *News & Observer* of Raleigh on March 5, 2016.

A quick note about the Campaign for Real Barbecue, the effort to celebrate barbecue places that cook on nothing but wood. The campaign has chapters in North and South Carolina, Kentucky, and Georgia. I'm involved in the latter. I know that many restaurants using gas-assisted smokers produce good barbecue, but it seems to me that we ought to recognize the ones that still do it the old way.

Chapter 3. Big Feeds

Much of this chapter is drawn from a talk I gave about barbecue and politics at the 2002 Southern Foodways Alliance symposium at the University of Mississippi. The SFA published it in the anthology *Cornbread Nation 2: The United States of Barbecue*, edited by Lolis Eric Elie (University of North Carolina Press, 2004).

The Jack Walton inaugural barbecue was covered by the *Daily Oklahoman* and the *New York Times* and was the subject of a lively academic article by William Warren Rogers in the Spring 1997 issue of *Chronicles of Oklahoma*.

The Walt Whitman parody "The Song of the Barbecue" appeared on September 29, 1860, in *Vanity Fair*. The barbecue groves on the Capitol grounds are described in *The Papers of Frederick Law Olmsted: The Early Boston Years, 1882–1890* (Johns Hopkins University Press, 2013).

I found an account of the 1895 encampment of the Grand Army of the Republic in *The Encyclopedia of Louisville*, edited by John E. Kleber (University Press of Kentucky, 2001). The *Washington Post* covered the reconciliation barbecue at Chickamauga on September 29, 1889. The Klan barbecue in Indiana comes from *Notre Dame vs. The Klan* by Todd Tucker (Loyola Press, 2004). Daniel Vaughn wrote about Klan barbecues in Texas in "Barbekue," an essay in the Summer 2018 issue of the SFA journal *Gravy*. The Denver barbecue melee was a front-page story in the *Rocky Mountain News* on January, 28, 1898.

Huey Long's barbecue radio address was collected in *Webster's Guide to American History* (Merriam-Webster, 1971). William Anderson wrote about the Talmadges and their legendary campaign barbecues in *The Wild Man from Sugar Creek* (Louisiana State University Press, 1975). Marvin Griffin's lament about losing an election in Georgia became such a well-known quote that it was the title of Scott E. Buchanan's biography of him: *Some of the People Who Ate My Barbecue Didn't Vote for Me* (Vanderbilt University Press, 2011).

The detail about FDR's death and the barbecue he never got to attend comes from *Franklin D. Roosevelt: The War Years, 1939–1945* by Roger Daniels (University of Illinois Press, 2016). The story about John F. Kennedy and the LBJ Ranch barbecue comes from oral histories at the Lyndon B. Johnson Library and Museum. Johnson wasn't the last president to host a barbecue summit in Texas; George W. Bush had one for Russian president Vladimir Putin in 2001, two months after 9/11.

The Atlanta newspapers ran through barrels of ink printing stories about the possum banquet for President Taft. The Atlanta History Center has a menu from the evening, which shows that many more conventional dishes were also served. Incidentally, Taft isn't the only president who has consumed varmint 'cue. In a 2009 profile of Bill Clinton, the *New York Times Magazine* quoted the former president joking about the annual raccoon supper he attended as governor of Arkansas. "Until you have eaten barbecued coon," he said, "you have not lived."

Chapter 4. South by Southwest

Texas barbecue is too big for one book. I consulted several of them: *The Prophets of Smoked Meat* by Daniel Vaughn (HarperCollins, 2013), *Republic of Barbecue* by Elizabeth S. D. Englehardt (University of Texas Press, 2009), *Texas BBQ* by Wyatt McSpadden (University of Texas Press, 2009), and *Legends of Texas Barbecue Cookbook* by Robb Walsh (Chronicle, 2002).

Walsh considered the roots of Texas barbecue in a talk he gave at the 2002 SFA symposium, collected in *Cornbread Nation 2*. He writes about Texas barbecue history frequently on his website (www.robbwalsh.com). *Texas Monthly*'s site (www.tmbbq.com) has a wealth of information about Lone Star barbecue. When Vaughn was hired as the magazine's barbecue editor, it rated a feature in the *New York Times* on March 23, 2013.

Vaughn wrote about Walter Jetton, LBJ's barbecue man, in a post on July 23, 2015, linking to a memorial page maintained by Jetton's grandson, Chris Jetton (www.jettons.jacjam.com). The story of Kreuz Market and Smitty's was based on a *Texas Monthly* article in February 1999 and other media accounts, on an interview I did with Jim Sells, and on an SFA oral history with Rick Schmidt. The *New York Times*'s Manny Fernandez wrote about the waiting line at Franklin Barbecue on January 27, 2016.

As for that other ranch barbecue, the Santa Maria style in California, the most complete article I read was Margo True's "The West's Best Unsung BBQ Town" in the August 2013 *Sunset*.

One more thing: Chris Elley's 2004 documentary film *Barbecue: A Texas Love Story* is a hoot. Among its many quotable lines is this one from singer Kinky Friedman: "Jesus loved barbecue. That's pretty well known."

Chapter 5. Pig Sandwiches

Leonard's, once the largest barbecue restaurant in Memphis (and maybe anywhere), is well documented in books and newspapers. I interviewed the owner, Dan Brown, and read several oral histories related to his and other barbecue places conducted for the SFA. Craig David Meek's *Memphis Barbecue: A Succulent History of Smoke, Sauce & Soul* (History Press, 2014) deals with the development of the city's barbecue restaurants in great detail. I also consulted Susan Puckett's *Eat Drink Delta: A Hungry Traveler's Journey through the Soul of the South* (University of Georgia Press, 2013), which describes Memphis dining as well as the Delta culture that nurtured it.

For the early history of barbecue clubs and restaurants, Moss's *Barbecue* was a good source. The clubs I mention in Atlanta were featured in the *Atlanta Constitution* on May 17, 1891, and May 20, 1898. I first learned about

shows Ellsworth B. A. Zwoyer's 1897 application as the earliest for making charcoal briquettes. Scores of other charcoal innovations have received patents since then.

As for beer-can chicken, I heard Craig Goldwyn debunk it at the Decatur Book Festival in 2016 and read about it in his 2016 book *Meathead: The Science of Great Barbecue and Grilling* (Houghton Mifflin Harcourt, 2016).

Chapter 8. The Color of 'cue

I read about Will Hill, the man who informed the makers of *Gone with the Wind* about plantation barbecues, in the Wilbur G. Kurtz Sr. Papers at the Atlanta History Center's Kenan Research Center. Kurtz's wife, Annie Laurie Fuller Kurtz, visited the set in California and wrote features about it for the *Atlanta Constitution*, including an April 2, 1939, account of the day the Twelve Oaks barbecue was staged far from the cotton fields of Georgia at Busch Gardens in Pasadena.

I spoke with Jessica B. Harris about why enslaved Africans might have taken to making barbecue so readily. Wesley Jones's recollection of antebellum barbecues came from the *Slave Narratives*, volume 14, *South Carolina*, conducted by the Federal Writers' Project in the late 1930s. The insurrections plotted at barbecues are described in *Gabriel's Rebellion: The Virginia Slave Conspiracies of 1800 and 1802* by Douglas R. Egerton (University of North Carolina Press, 1993) and in *Nat Turner: A Slave Rebellion in History and Memory*, edited by Kenneth S. Greenberg (Oxford University Press, 2003). The *New York Times* published an account of the emancipation barbecue in South Carolina on January 9, 1863.

Harper's Weekly ran a cover illustration of men tending the barbecue pits at the Atlanta exposition on November 9, 1895. Bobby Seale has talked about his uncle's barbecue place in Texas and its quasi integration in numerous interviews and in his book *Barbeque'n with Bobby* (Ten Speed, 1988). The vignette about white folks eating at a black barbecue place in Alabama ran in the *Afro-American* of Baltimore on April 8, 1933.

The saga of Ollie's Barbecue and desegregation was told by Michael Durham in *Life* magazine on October 9, 1964, in the book *Civil Rights and Public Accommodations* by Richard C. Cortner (University Press of Kansas, 2001), and in an oral history with Ollie McClung Jr. conducted by Joan Hoffman for the University of Alabama, Birmingham, in 1975. Jack Hitt recounted Maurice Bessinger's history of resistance in a story for the *New York Times Magazine*, "A Confederacy of Sauces," on August 26, 2001. Bessinger explained his motivations in his 2001 memoir, *Defending My Heritage*. Kathleen Purvis wrote a sensitive story about going back to Maurice's Piggie Park for the first time in years in the *Charlotte Observer* on December 8, 2016. Lauren Collins's "America's Most Political Food," about

Bessinger's family and their efforts to overcome their father's reputation, appeared in the *New Yorker* of April 24, 2017.

I've spoken with Michael Twitty several times about his belief that African American contributions to barbecue have been downplayed and heard him speak about the subject during a Juneteenth program at the Atlanta History Center and again when his book, *The Cooking Gene*, was published in 2017. His provocative column in the *Guardian* ran on July 4, 2015. I've interviewed Adrian Miller, Carolyn Wells, Flora Payne, and Moe Cason about their experiences. Cason was profiled in the *New Yorker* of September 6, 2014, and Miller's commentary about the complexion of tv barbecue shows was posted on the sfa blog on June 20, 2012.

Taylor Branch talked about Martin Luther King Jr., Gandhi, and barbecue in *Smithsonian* magazine in January 2015. The involvement of barbecue restaurants in the civil rights movement has been covered by Jim Shahin in the *Washington Post* on February 22 and September 19, 2016, and by Meredith Bethune in the sfa publication *Gravy*'s Fall 2016 issue. Pamela Alexander, the daughter of the man who founded Aleck's Barbecue Heaven, refreshed my memory about that late, lamented rib shack in an oral history I conducted for the Atlanta History Center in November 2017. Andrew Young told me about King writing speeches over barbecue ribs. During our interview, Young also remembered one night not long before the 1996 Olympics began in Atlanta when he had to go to an emergency room with chest pains; turned out he was only suffering indigestion from overindulging in ribs. "I can't eat them like I used to," he said. "I'm sort of a one-rib man now."

Chapter 9. Of Pits and Poets

This chapter was great fun to research. I could have made it two or three times longer with literary allusions to barbecue alone, but I didn't want to disappear into Google Books and never be heard from again. Some specific sources are worth mentioning.

I learned about Anthony Philip Heinrich and "The Barbecue Divertimento" from several sources, including *America's Music: From the Pilgrims to the Present* by Gilbert Chase (University of Illinois Press, 1987). In a completely different vein, I highly recommend *Barbecue Any Old Time*, the compilation of vintage blues songs about eating meat from Old Hat Records (www.oldhatrecords.com).

Several books provided information about artists who depicted barbecue in their works: *African-American Artists, 1929–1945: Prints, Drawings, and Paintings in the Metropolitan Museum of Art* (Yale University Press, 2003), *Archibald Motley: Jazz Age Modernist* by Richard J. Powell (Duke University Press, 2014), and *The Other Side of Color: African-American*

Art in the Collection of Camille O. and William H. Cosby Jr. by David C. Driskell (Pomegranate, 2001).

John Steinbeck was barbecuing spareribs at his home in New York City when a reporter with the *Oakland Tribune* came to interview him on October 18, 1953. The letter in which Tennessee Williams mentions working at the Pig 'n Whistle in Macon, Georgia, is found in *The Selected Letters of Tennessee Williams*, vol. 1, *1920–1945* (New Directions, 2000). According to some sources, the rock 'n' roller Little Richard worked at the same restaurant a few years later. That's an awful lot of drama for one barbecue joint.

Chapter 10. Sauced

Much of the information for this chapter came from reporting I did for *The Ultimate Barbecue Sauce Cookbook* (Longstreet Press, 1995), which I wrote with Susan Puckett, the longtime food editor of the *Atlanta Journal-Constitution*. I've kept up with the subject because I'm a hopeless saucehead.

The ad for the Georgia Barbecue Sauce Company first ran in the *Atlanta Constitution* on January 31, 1909, and turns up at least seventeen more times in the next three months. Scott's Barbecue Sauce, the quintessential Carolina vinegar sauce, figures in *Adam's Ribs: The Success Story of Adam Scott, the Barbecue King*, written and published by Moses Roundtree in 1977.

Evander Holyfield, Richard Petty, and William "the Fridge" Perry are far from the only sports stars to get into the barbecue business. Boxer George Foreman made a fortune from his little electric grills. Baseball star Boog Powell opened barbecue stands in Ocean City, Maryland, and at the Baltimore Orioles ballpark. Hall of Fame pitcher Nolan Ryan came out with *The Nolan Ryan Beef & Barbecue Cookbook* in 2014. Football great Billy Sims went into franchising in Oklahoma and opened more than forty Billy Sims Barbecue restaurants in five states. On a sadder note, the Shoeless Joe Jackson Museum in Greenville, South Carolina, says that Jackson opened a barbecue place there after he was kicked out of major league baseball for his part in the conspiracy to fix the 1919 World Series. He went from barbecue to running a liquor store.

Chapter 11. Trophies as Tall as Steers

The Kaiser Foil Cookout Championship was advertised in the *Life* magazine issue of June 29, 1959. *Sports Illustrated* covered the event in its July 20, 1964, edition. Annette Erbeck, whose husband, Gail, won that year's grand prize, shared her recollections with me in an interview. Quick story: After her husband won, they were invited to sit at a private table with Joan Crawford, who ordered champagne but specified that it be served in water tumblers. "She said she didn't want to buy Champagne for all the other contestants," Erbeck told me. "I think there was something to *Mommie Dearest*."

My census of barbecue contests comes from the organizations that sanction them. Calvin Trillin wrote about the burgeoning competitive barbecue circuit in the *New Yorker* of August 12, 1985. *Memphis* magazine documented the early days of the Memphis in May championship in May 2006. Other details about the contest come from the *Memphis Flyer* newspaper, from Memphis in May, from my own visits to the contest, and from interviews with competitors, including founding members of the Redneck Bar-B-Q Express team. Myron Mixon, star of *BBQ Pitmasters*, showed his swagger in *Smokin' with Myron Mixon* (Ballantine, 2011).

My history of the Kansas City Barbeque Society comes from conversations with Carolyn Wells, Ardie Davis, and others, and from its entertaining publication, the *BullSheet*. About judging classes: after I became a Certified Barbeque Judge, I learned that there were higher degrees of training—Master Barbeque Judge, et cetera—and I noticed that some people wear their multiple certification tags like a chestful of military medals. That's the way it is with barbecue: you can always take it to another level.

Chapter 12. A World of Barbecue

John T. Edge wrote about the phenomenon of Korean barbecue tacos in the *New York Times* on July 26, 2010. Bigmista's Barbecue and the Kogi BBQ Taco truck have been covered widely (especially the latter) in the Los Angeles media. I read about both in *Los Angeles Street Food* by Farley Elliott (History Press, 2015).

Bill Addison and John Kessler wrote about Heirloom Market BBQ when they were the dining critics at *Atlanta* magazine and the *Atlanta Journal-Constitution*, respectively. Addison included Heirloom's spicy Korean-style pork barbecue sandwich in his "23 Essential Barbecue Dishes in America" for the website *Eater* on June 7, 2016.

To get an idea how American barbecue has spread around the world, I did searches for barbecue restaurants in several dozen cities. While a surprising number of hits turned up, there were a few false positives. Searching Mumbai, for instance, I saw an Indian chain of sixty restaurants called Barbeque Nation, but they seem unrelated to classic barbecue except in name. Jim Shahin, visiting the Beast, the Texas-inspired restaurant in Paris, wrote about U.S. barbecue going international for the *Washington Post* on January 19, 2016.

The barbecue pilgrims from Red's True BBQ in Britain blogged about their trip to Alabama and Houston at www.truebarbecue.com. I learned about Braai Day from several news sources, including National Public

Radio ("Braai Day Aims to Bring S. Africans Together over Barbecue," August 26, 2013).

Monique Truong's love letter to Red Bridges Barbecue Lodge was delivered at the 2012 Southern Foodways symposium and reprinted in the *Washington Post* on November 30, 2012, and in the anthology *Cornbread Nation 7* (University of Georgia Press, 2014).

Epilogue

I realized how long people have been talking about the demise of barbecue when I ran across a decades-old article by Ralph McGill, the revered editor of my alma mater, the *Atlanta Constitution*. McGill was a Tennesseean who felt strongly about southern food and often wrote about biscuits, Brunswick stew, and the like when he wasn't wrestling with race relations and political affairs. In "What's Wrong with Southern Cooking?"—a freelance piece he did on March 26, 1949, for the *Saturday Evening Post*—he lambasted the restaurants trying to lure unsuspecting tourists with dubious fried chicken and suspicious barbecue, making them sound like the road-food equivalent of a speed trap.

"Regarding barbecue," he wrote, "perhaps the best advice is to eat none of it unless it is vouched for by one acquainted with the local situation. And then only if he seems to be an honest follow. It is apt not to be barbecue at all, but half-done pork, slices of which are lathered with a hot sauce. . . . What the average tourist gets is something which rests on the stomach like a fricassee made of old political-campaign speeches."

The lead illustration shows a lurid landscape of neon signs for clichéd southern restaurants, including a lit-up pig called The Li'l Ol' Greasy Hawg Bar-B-Q. Maybe I'm easy, but the sight of that imagined sign made me want to try the Li'l Ol' Greasy Hawg's chopped-pork sandwich. You never know.

SELECTED BIBLIOGRAPHY

You won't notice many cookbooks here. There are a world of excellent barbecue cookbooks, but this listing focuses on volumes that tell the story of barbecue and the larger forces that shaped its development. I wish my name didn't come first, but that's the alphabet for you.

Auchmutey, Jim, and Susan Puckett. *The Ultimate Barbecue Sauce Cookbook*. Atlanta: Longstreet, 1995.

Berry, Wes. *The Kentucky Barbecue Book*. Lexington: University Press of Kentucky, 2013.

Bessinger, Maurice. *Defending My Heritage*. West Columbia, S.C.: Lmbone-Lehone, 2001.

Caldwell, Wilber W. *Searching for the Dixie Barbecue: Journeys into the Southern Psyche*. Sarasota, Fla.: Pineapple Press, 2005.

Cortner, Richard C. *Civil Rights and Public Accommodations: The Heart of Atlanta Motel and McClung Cases*. Lawrence: University of Kansas Press, 2001.

Covey, Herbert C., and Dwight Eisnach. *What the Slaves Ate: Recollections of African American Foods and Foodways from the Slave Narratives*. Santa Barbara, Calif.: Greenwood, 2009.

Davis, Ardie A., Paul Kirk, and Carolyn Wells. *The Kansas City Barbeque Society Cookbook: Barbeque—It's Not Just for Breakfast Anymore*. 25th anniversary ed. Kansas City, Mo.: Andrews McMeel, 2010.

Deutsch, Jonathan, and Megan J. Elias. *Barbecue: A Global History*. London: Reaktion, 2014.

Edge, John T. *The Potlikker Papers: A Food History of the Modern South*. New York: Penguin, 2017.

Egerton, John. *Side Orders: Small Helpings of Southern Cookery & Culture*. Atlanta: Peachtree, 1990.

———. *Southern Food: At Home, on the Road, in History*. New York: Alfred A. Knopf, 1987.

Eighmey, Rae Katherine. *Abraham Lincoln in the Kitchen: A Culinary View of Lincoln's Life and Times*. Washington, D.C.: Smithsonian, 2013.

Elie, Lolis Eric., ed. *Cornbread Nation 2: The United States of Barbecue*. For the Southern Foodways Alliance. Chapel Hill: University of North Carolina Press, 2004.

———. *Smokestack Lightning: Adventures in the Heart of Barbecue Country*. New York: Farrar, Straus and Giroux, 1996.

Engelhardt, Elizabeth S. D. *Republic of Barbecue: Stories beyond the Brisket*. Austin: University of Texas Press, 2009.

Essig, Mark. *Lesser Beasts: A Snout-to-Tail History of the Humble Pig*. New York: Basic, 2015.

Ferris, Marcie Cohen. *The Edible South: The Power of Food and the Making of an American Region*. Chapel Hill: University of North Carolina Press, 2014.

Fertel, Rien. *The One True Barbecue: Fire, Smoke, and the Pitmasters Who Cook the Whole Hog*. New York: Touchstone, 2016.

Franklin, Aaron, and Jordan Mackay. *Franklin Barbecue: A Meat-Smoking Manifesto*. Berkeley, Calif.: Ten Speed Press, 2015.

Garner, Bob. *North Carolina Barbecue: Flavored by Time*. Winston-Salem, N.C.: John F. Blair, 1996.

Gelin, David Howard. *BBQ Joints: Stories and Secret Recipes from the Barbeque Belt*. Layton, Utah: Gibbs Smith, 2008.

Genovese, Eugene D. *Roll, Jordan, Roll: The World the Slaves Made*. New York: Pantheon, 1974.

Goldwyn, Meathead. *Meathead: The Science of Great Barbecue and Grilling*. Boston: Houghton Mifflin Harcourt, 2016.

Haddix, Carol Mighton, Bruce Kraig, and Colleen Taylor Sen, eds. *The Chicago Food Encyclopedia*. Urbana: University of Illinois Press, 2017.

Harris, Jessica B. *High on the Hog: A Culinary Journey from Africa to America*. New York: Bloomsbury, 2011.

———. *The Welcome Table: African-American Heritage Cooking*. New York: Simon and Schuster, 1995.

Haynes, Joseph R. *Virginia Barbecue: A History*. Charleston, S.C.: History Press, 2016.

Hernandez, Eddie, and Susan Puckett. *Turnip Greens & Tortillas: A Mexican Chef Spices Up the Southern Kitchen*. Boston: Houghton Mifflin Harcourt, 2018.

High, Lake E., Jr. *A History of South Carolina Barbeque*. Charleston, S.C.: History Press, 2013.

Hudson, Charles M. *Knights of Spain, Warriors of the Sun: Hernando de Soto and the South's Ancient Chiefdoms*. Athens: University of Georgia Press, 1997.

Hulton, Paul. *America 1585: The Complete Drawings of John White*. Chapel Hill: University of North Carolina Press, 1984.

Huntley, Dan, and Lisa Grace Lednicer. *Extreme Barbecue: Smokin' Rigs and Real Good Recipes*. San Francisco: Chronicle, 2007.

Johnson, Greg, and Vince Staten. *Real Barbecue*. New York: Harper & Row, 1988.

Johnson, Mark A. *An Irresistible History of Alabama Barbecue: From Wood Pit to White Sauce*. Charleston, S.C.: History Press, 2017.

Kuhne, Cecil C., III. *The Little Book of BBQ Law*. Chicago: American Bar Association, 2013.

Kurlansky, Mark. *The Food of a Younger Land*. New York: Riverhead, 2009.

Mariani, John. *America Eats Out: An Illustrated History of Restaurants, Taverns, Coffee Shops, Speakeasies, and Other Establishments That Have Fed Us for 350 Years*. New York: William Morrow, 1991.

McSpadden, Wyatt. *Texas BBQ*. Austin: University of Texas Press, 2009.

Meek, Craig David. *Memphis Barbecue: A Succulent History of Smoke, Sauce & Soul*. Charleston, S.C.: History Press, 2014.

Miller, Adrian. *Soul Food: The Surprising Story of an American Cuisine, One Plate at a Time*. Chapel Hill: University of North Carolina Press, 2013.

Miller, Tim. *Barbecue: A History*. Lanham, Md.: Rowman & Littlefield, 2014.

Moss, Robert F. *Barbecue: The History of an American Institution*. Tuscaloosa: University of Alabama Press, 2010.

Nealon, Tom. *Food Fights and Culture Wars: A Secret History of Taste*. London: British Library, 2016.

Neuhaus, Jessamyn. *Manly Meals and Mom's Home Cooking: Cookbooks and Gender in Modern America*. Baltimore: Johns Hopkins University Press, 2003.

Opie, Fred. *Zora Neale Hurston on Florida Food: Recipes, Remedies & Simple Pleasures*. Charleston, S.C.: History Press, 2015.

Puckett, Susan. *Eat Drink Delta: A Hungry Traveler's Journey through the Soul of the South*. Athens: University of Georgia Press, 2013.

Raichlen, Steven. *The Barbecue! Bible*. New York: Workman, 1998.

——. *Steven Raichlen's BBQ USA*, New York: Workman, 2003.

——. *Steven Raichlen's Planet Barbecue!* New York: Workman, 2010.

Reed, John Shelton. *Barbecue: A Savor the South Cookbook*. Chapel Hill: University of North Carolina Press, 2016.

Reed, John Shelton, and Dale Volberg Reed. *Holy Smoke: The Big Book of North Carolina Barbecue*. With William McKinney. Chapel Hill: University of North Carolina Press, 2008.

Sauceman, Fred W. *The Proffitts of Ridgewood: An Appalachian Family's Life in Barbecue*. Macon, Ga.: Mercer University Press, 2017.

Seale, Bobby. *Barbeque'n with Bobby: Righteous, Down-home Barbeque Recipes by Bobby Seale.* Berkeley, Calif.: Ten Speed Press, 1988.

Sherman, Sean. *The Sioux Chef's Indigenous Kitchen.* With Beth Dooley. Minneapolis: University of Minnesota Press, 2017.

Stokes, Ashli Quesinberry, and Wendy Atkins-Sayre. *Consuming Identity: The Role of Food in Redefining the South.* Jackson: University Press of Mississippi, 2016.

Sunset. Sunset's Barbecue Book. San Francisco: Lane Publishing, 1938.

Tesene, R. H. *Santa Maria Style Barbecue.* Los Olivos, Calif.: Olive Press, 1997.

Thorne, John. *Serious Pig: An American Cook in Search of His Roots.* With Matt Lewis Thorne. New York: North Point Press, 1996.

Tipton-Martin, Toni. *The Jemima Code: Two Centuries of African American Cookbooks.* Austin: University of Texas Press, 2015.

Trillin, Calvin. *The Tummy Trilogy.* New York: Farrar, Straus and Giroux, 1994.

Twitty, Michael W. *The Cooking Gene: A Journey through African American Culinary History in the Old South.* New York: HarperCollins, Amistad, 2017.

Vaughn, Daniel. *The Prophets of Smoked Meat: A Journey through Texas Barbecue.* New York: Anthony Bourdain/Ecco, 2013.

Walsh, Robb. *Barbecue Crossroads: Notes and Recipes from a Southern Odyssey.* Austin: University of Texas Press, 2013.

———. *Legends of Texas Barbecue Cookbook: Recipes and Recollections from the Pit Bosses.* San Francisco: Chronicle, 2002.

Warnes, Andrew. *Savage Barbecue: Race, Culture, and the Invention of America's First Food.* Athens: University of Georgia Press, 2008.

Weatherford, Jack. *Indian Givers: How the Indians of the Americas Transformed the World.* New York: Crown, 1988.

Wilkerson, Isabel. *The Warmth of Other Suns: The Epic Story of America's Great Migration.* New York: Random House, 2010.

Witzel, Michael Karl. *Barbecue Road Trip: Recipes, Restaurants & Pitmasters from America's Great Barbecue Regions.* Minneapolis: Voyageur, 2008.

Worgul, Doug. *The Grand Barbecue: A Celebration of the History, Places, Personalities and Techniques of Kansas City Barbecue.* Kansas City, Mo.: Kansas City Star Books, 2001.

CREDITS

Images

23 (top left)	Jim Auchmutey
23 (bottom left)	Brunswick Downtown Development Authority
23 (right)	University of Kentucky Archives
27	Library of Congress
28	Raymond Steth, American, 1916–97, *Southern Barbecue*, c. 1940–42, lithograph, sheet 9×11⅝ inches, Saint Louis Art Museum, Gift of the Federal Works Agency, Work Progress Administration 320: 1943. Courtesy of St. Louis Museum of Art
29	Ed Reilly Collection
30 (both)	Jim Auchmutey
32	Jim Auchmutey
33	Original artwork by Phil Blank for the Southern Foodways Alliance
35	Library of Congress. Photo by Jack Delano
36	Fort Sill Museum Collection, OHS item #19580.1, courtesy of Oklahoma Historical Society
39 (left)	Virginia Museum of History & Culture Library
39 (right)	Henry R. Robinson, *The Political Barbecue*, 1834. Library of Congress
40	*Frank Leslie's Magazine*, North Wind Picture Archives / Alamy
42 (top)	Courtesy of Anthony Hodges. Photo by Reid Laurens
42 (bottom)	Library of Congress
43	Albert and Shirley Small Special Collections Library, University of Virginia Archives
44	National Photo Co., Library of Congress
46 (top left)	Chadwick History Museum
46 (top right)	*Washington Bee*
46 (bottom left)	University Archives, Special Collections and Archives, Georgia State University, Atlanta
46 (bottom right)	Courtesy of the Bancroft Library, University of California, Berkeley
47 (top)	Courtesy of State Archives of Florida, Florida Memory
47 (bottom left)	Mallard Creek Presbyterian Church
47 (bottom right)	Author's collection
48	James G. Kenan Research Center at the Atlanta History Center
49	Courtesy of State Archives of Florida, Florida Memory
50	Ed Valdez_HP / © Houston Chronicle. Used with permission
52	Photo by Thomas J. O'Halloran, *U.S. News and World Report*. Library of Congress

54	Ed Reilly Collection
56	Wyatt McSpadden
59	Photograph by Carly Kocurek for the Southern Foodways Alliance
60 (top)	Jim Auchmutey
60 (bottom)	Courtesy, W. D. Smith Commercial Photography Collections, Special Collections, the University of Texas at Arlington Library, Arlington, Texas
61	Ed Reilly Collection
62	General Photograph Collection, University of Texas at San Antonio Libraries Special Collections
63 (both)	Jim Auchmutey
64	Jim Auchmutey
65 (both)	Ed Reilly Collection
66	Ed Reilly Collection
68	Photo by Russell Lee. Farm Security Administration, Library of Congress
70 (left)	Doug Mills / *New York Times* / Redux
70 (right)	Sonny Bryan's Smokehouse
71	Archival Services, University Libraries, the University of Akron
72	Photograph by Rien T. Fertel for the Southern Foodways Alliance
75	Photo by Marion Post Wolcott. Farm Security Administration, Library of Congress
76	Fresh Air Bar-B-Que
77	Jim Auchmutey
78	Ed Reilly Collection
80	Leonard's Barbecue
81	Items from Leonard's Barbecue. Photo by Jim Auchmutey
82	Original McDonald's Site and Museum
83	Dickey's
84 (top)	Robert Moss
84 (bottom)	Photo by John Hensel. Courtesy of South Caroliniana Library, University of South Carolina, Columbia, S.C.
85 (top)	Ed Reilly Collection
85 (bottom)	Photo by Jim Warren. Courtesy of Melissa Warren.
86	Jim Auchmutey
87	Rendezvous Lounge
88 (top)	Ed Reilly Collection
88 (center)	Ardie A. Davis Collection
88 (bottom)	Ed Reilly Collection
89 (top & center)	Ardie A. Davis Collection

89 (bottom)	Evansville Public Library / James and Rosemary Geiss Collection
90	*Kansas City Sun*, January 5, 1918
92	Jim Auchmutey
93	Jacob Lawrence. *The Migration Series, Panel 1* (1940–41), casein tempera on hardboard, 12 x 18 in. © 2016 The Jacob and Gwendolyn Knight Lawrence Foundation, Seattle / Artists Rights Society (ARS), New York
94	© Rene Burri / Magnum Photos
95	Courtesy of East Bay Dragons
97	Photograph by Lisa Powell for the Southern Foodways Alliance
98 (both)	Photograph by Amy C. Evans for the Southern Foodways Alliance
102	Jackson County Historical Society Archives, WC 55424B
104	Gates Barbecue. Photo by Reid Laurens
105	From the *Kansas City Star*, December 30, 1982, © 1982 McClatchy. All rights reserved. Used by permission and protected by the copyright laws of the United States. The printing, copying, redistruction, or retransmission of this content without express written permission is prohibited
106	Ed Reilly Collection
107	Matchbooks from Ed Reilly Collection
108	*Sunset Magazine*
110	From *I Love Lucy*, "Building a Bar-B-Q," 1957. CBS Corporation Photo Archive / Getty Images
111	Ed Reilly Collection
113 (both)	Ed Reilly Collection
114	Char-Broil LLC and the W. C. Bradley Co.
115	Ed Reilly Collection
116 (both)	Ed Reilly Collection
117	Atlanta History Center
118 (top)	Ed Reilly Collection
118 (bottom)	Library of Congress
119	Perry Barlow / *The New Yorker*. © Condé Nast
120 (all)	Ed Reilly Collection
121	Jim Auchmutey
123 (top)	Photo by Maurice Johnson. Courtesy National Park Service, Dwight D. Eisenhower Presidential Library & Museum
123 (bottom)	Ed Reilly Collection
125	Ed Reilly Collection
126	Ed Reilly Collection
127	Ed Reilly Collection

128	Ed Reilly Collection
129 (both)	Ed Reilly Collection
130	Jim Auchmutey
132 (left)	Licensed by Warner Bros. Entertainment Inc. All rights reserved
132 (right)	James G. Kenan Research Center at the Atlanta History Center
134	Federal Writer's Project, Library of Congress
135 (left)	W. A. Rogers, "Turning the Meat—a Georgia Barbecue at the Atlanta Exposition," cover of *Harper's Weekly*, November 9, 1895. Ed Reilly Collection
135 (right)	Vanishing Georgia, Georgia Archives, University System of Georgia
136	Ed Reilly Collection
139 (left)	Stuart A. Rose Manuscript, Archives, and Rare Book Library, Emory University
139 (right)	© Al Clayton. Used with permission of Al Clayton Photography LLC
140	Peter McKee
141 (top)	*Birmingham News* / Barcroft Media
141 (bottom)	Postcard from author's collection
142	Ed Reilly Collection
143	Jim Auchmutey
145	Photo by Claus Peuckert, courtesy of Moe Cason
147	Pamela Alexander
148	*Parade Magazine*
150	Old Hat Records
151	Old Hat Records
152	Ed Reilly Collection
153 (top)	*Atlanta Constitution*
153 (bottom)	Alan Lomax Collection, Library of Congress
155	Licensed by Warner Bros. Entertainment. All Rights Reserved.
156	Author's collection
157	John Baeder, *Col. Poole's Pig Hill of Fame*, 1995, oil on canvas, Morris Museum of Art, Augusta, Georgia. Purchase made possible by the Passailaigue Acquisitions Fund. © 1995 John Baeder
159	Warner Bros.
160	Author's collection
161	Ed Reilly Collection. Photo by Reid Laurens
162	Author's collection
164	Author's collection
168	Author's collection

Recipes

124 From Jim Shahin, Smoke Signals column in the *Washington Post*. Courtesy of Jim Shahin.

138 From Michael W. Twitty, *The Cooking Gene* (New York: Amistad Press, 2017). Courtesy of Michael Twitty.

169 By Jim Auchmutey.

175 Courtesy of Chris Lilly, Big Bob Gibson's Barbecue—Decatur, Alabama.

178 From Jim Auchmutey and Susan Puckett, *The Ultimate Barbecue Sauce Cookbook* (Atlanta: Longstreet Press, 1995).

180 From Jim Auchmutey and Susan Puckett, *The Ultimate Barbecue Sauce Cookbook* (Atlanta: Longstreet Press, 1995).

189 Courtesy of Brad Erbeck.

196 Courtesy of Melissa Cookston.

212 Courtesy of Heirloom Market BBQ—Atlanta, Georgia.

217 From Jim Auchmutey and Susan Puckett, *The Ultimate Barbecue Sauce Cookbook* (Atlanta: Longstreet Press, 1995).

218 Courtesy of Eric Vernon and the Bar-B-Q Shop.

INDEX